T0248207

Low-Hanging Fruit

Also by Randy Rainbow

Playing with Myself

Low-Hanging Fruit

Sparkling Whines, Champagne Problems, and
Pressing Issues from My Gay Agenda

Randy Rainbow

ST. MARTIN'S PRESS
NEW YORK

First published in the United States by St. Martin's Press,
an imprint of St. Martin's Publishing Group

www.stmartins.com

Designed by Devan Norman
Cherry illustration © vector toon / Shutterstock

The Library of Congress Cataloging-in-Publication Data is available
upon request.

ISBN 978-1-250-32714-7 (hardcover)
ISBN 978-1-250-32715-4 (ebook)

Our books may be purchased in bulk for promotional, educational, or
business use. Please contact your local bookseller or the Macmillan
Corporate and Premium Sales Department at 1-800-221-7945, extension 5442,
or by email at MacmillanSpecialMarkets@macmillan.com.

First Edition: 2024

10 9 8 7 6 5 4 3 2 1

For anyone who has ever aggravated, irritated, antagonized, dismissed, offended, harassed, diminished, provoked, peeved, angered, annoyed, riled, disturbed, miffed, vexed, irked, crossed, or wronged me in any way . . .

I forgive you.

Contents

Low-Hanging Fruit

Letter of Resignation

Dear Stupid People,

Please accept this letter as formal notification that I am hereby resigning from trying to fix you, effective immediately.

While I have appreciated the opportunity to serve my country and the human race at large by attempting to correct your every social infraction and flawed thought process during my self-appointed tenure, the undertaking has become an exhausting and time-consuming hindrance to my peace and mental well-being.

Therefore, I have reached the decision to relieve myself of all responsibilities associated with the job, including but not limited to responding to your misguided ignorance, rectifying your gross ineptitude, and critiquing or even questioning your egregious insensitivity and lack of common sense.

From now on, when you board a subway car on which I am already seated and decide for some curious reason to settle into a seat disturbingly close to—or directly next to—mine, even though said subway car is otherwise empty and there are acres of uncharted mismatched orange plastic on either side for us both to spread out in comfortably, I will henceforth no longer glare at you disapprovingly for eleven stops. I might even scoot a little closer and rest my head on your shoulder.

Going forward, if I tell a joke that intensely offends and out-rages you, either because you sincerely don't comprehend it or you simply have nothing else on your calendar that day, I regret-tably will be unavailable to explain my joke to you. You will need to navigate those waters alone, and I wish you the best. If this is an emergency, please hang up and dial 911. (Note: Please do not actually dial 911. That was a joke.)

If I hold a door for you—a perfect stranger—as we both leave a restaurant or other such establishment, and you don't say "Thank you" or even acknowledge my existence as you ever-so-slowly walk past me like you're leisurely roaming the Louvre on a lazy af-ternoon . . . please have a wonderful day, and I hope you enjoyed this free service. I will most certainly not be cursing you in my shower later that evening while fantasizing what I wish I had said to you in the moment. My schedule will simply no longer allow it.

To those of you who find it necessary to talk, sing, eat, text, endlessly clear your throat, snore, fidget, burp, fart, or file your in-come taxes while in the audience of a concert or Broadway show, today is your lucky day. Though I may reluctantly spend $475 on a ticket to a musical version of *Don't Tell Mom the Babysitter's Dead* only to listen to you and your spouse deliberate over the lasagna you had for dinner, nevermore will I disturb you with my pesky admonishments for such behavior.

If you should visit Manhattan's Central Park for a jog or stroll and insist on ignoring the pedestrian icons painted strategically along the track for your convenience and safety, it is my pleasure to inform you that you may now do so freely. I will no longer murmur expletives in your general direction when you inevitably and violently crash into me. What's more, when I see you charging toward me like a rabid bat out of hell with that blissfully vacant expression that comes from the confidence of knowing that you are the world's only living occupant, I will no longer encroach on your rightful territory. I will instead leap into the nearest tree to clear your path as you pass, clutch a branch, and tip my bird-shit-covered hat to you with due deference as squirrels gnaw at my bloody knuckles.

Should you walk at a sloth's pace through areas of heavy foot traffic or busy intersections with your face buried in your iPhone, seemingly unaware of the hundreds of people surrounding you, the time has come for me to explore opportunities other than screaming, "GET OFF YOUR PHONE, ASSHOLE, THERE'S A CAR COMING!" Good luck, and please let me know what assistance I can offer during this transitional period.

Attention those of you who see nothing problematic about removing your shoes and socks on an airplane and resting your dried, cracked winter hooves that look like they require immediate medical attention, never mind a pedicure, on the seat in front of you—or, God forbid, hanging them over the headrest of the seat in front of you: I will no longer hold myself responsible for judging you for the remainder of our trip or ask the flight attendant if it would be possible to zip-tie you and lock you in an overhead bin until you can be properly detained and arrested upon arrival. Instead, I will politely continue about my own business, watching episodes of *Real Housewives* while trying not to vomit, and hoping for the plane to crash.

If you allow absurd conspiracy theories and AI-generated imagery circulating in your social media feed to inform your political and sociological ideologies, consider this my eternal out-of-office reply. Thank you for flagging that clearly deepfake video of Barack Obama casually confessing to eating live human babies in a very public forum. I'm currently away from trying to convince you to use whatever brainpower you may have left but will be sure to review it once I return . . . never.

If someone with an unverified profile and two followers claiming to be me on Instagram reaches out to confide in you that I am actually a Nigerian prince in disguise desperately in need of your credit-card information so I can regain access to my frozen bank account and share my royal fortune with you, go ahead and type in that CVC code, babe. Please do not contact me directly. I am hereby relinquishing any obligation to dissuade you from being ridiculous.

Additionally, on the topic of social media, should you take pleasure in relentlessly (and anonymously) taunting me on numerous platforms for being what you refer to as "too woke" because of my quirky distaste for injustice while you continue to elect deranged criminals and ingest bigoted propaganda from pretend news organizations, I will no longer contend. In fact, I will oblige you and go back to sleep.

If you are vehemently outspoken about your opposition to participating in certain types of wedding ceremonies, reading certain books, and attending Disney films with color-blind casting or performances where men may be dressed as women lip-synching to Shania Twain because you view these things as existential crises, please note that today was my very last day to tell you that you may absolutely feel free to fuck off and live whatever life your cold heart desires just so long as you don't infringe upon mine. Yay! Let's have some cake.

I hope this message finds you well, people who don't believe in science yet claim to know more about it than actual scientists and health officials on the grounds that you follow Scott Baio on Twitter (or X, or whatever the hell it's called now). I have left the keys to our future with reception. Take care! Wishing you and yours a very happy, plague-infested, postapocalyptic holiday season.

From this time forth, I will no longer resist your incessant predilection for Zoom meetings, even though the content of such meetings could usually be summed up efficiently in a brief note that would take you less time to compose than it did to send the Zoom link. While it was once my duty to protest, I will now passively sit and listen to you drone on about business services and functions you never actually intend to perform, all the while endeavoring to not let my facial expressions reveal that with every word you speak, all life force is slowly draining from my body.

Finally, if you feel entitled, or even obligated, to utilize the FaceTime feature (without use of AirPods or headphones, no less) every time you call a friend or family member in public, making it impossible for the rest of us to avoid not only one but both excruciatingly banal sides of your inane conversation . . . do carry on! The fact remains that simply because technology exists, you are not granted free rein to use it all the time, particularly if it's disruptive to others. I mean, just because I love my cordless Philips Norelco body-hair trimmer, it doesn't give me the right to walk around the produce department at Trader Joe's shaving my ass. Nevertheless, it is no longer my responsibility to remind you of this. I am officially off the clock.

I understand that as a fellow inhabitant of this planet with no immediate plans for relocation, the option of avoiding one another entirely is impractical. It has also recently been brought to my attention that you are reproducing at an alarming rate. In the inevitable event that our paths cross again, please rest assured that I will act professionally and courteously but very much look forward to never working with you again.

Yours no longer,

Randy Rainbow

Bye, gurl.

2

Gurl, You're a Karen

When my literary agent asked me what I thought the theme of my next book should be, I told him that as a respected commentator with my finger on the pulse of public discourse and the current social climate, I strongly intuited that what people really want more of right now is privileged white males complaining about shit. I'll never forget his response: "Randy," he said, "I have to take another call." I never heard back from him. And don't you worry . . . I have already complained to management.

The truth is, I have a lot of complaints about a lot of things. Some of my closest friends and family might even call me a whiner, a nag, a nitpicker, or a kvetch. Fuck those people . . . I never liked them anyway. I was raised to believe there are simply right and wrong ways to do just about everything, from loading the dishwasher to running the country. Yes, even something as seemingly inconsequential as eating a peanut-butter cup can be done the wrong way, despite the lies and propaganda being sold to you by Big Reese's. When people insist on choosing the wrong way—be it for lack of care, sheer laziness, nefarious intent, or any other reason—I take exception.

You might view this as a binary way of thinking, especially from someone many presume to be nonbinary, but allow me to push back against that criticism, dear reader. I argue that it's absolutely the *right* way of thinking. How do I know this for a fact, you ask? Because it's what I think. Now, pipe down, over there! I mean, who's writing this book . . . you or me?

In the age of "the Karen," the act of complaining has become intensely stigmatized. The time-honored tradition—dare I say art—of the complaint is now an endangered one. And before I go on presenting this vitally important albeit half-baked case in defense of complaining, I wish to state that I am in no way endorsing the kind associated with the aforementioned pejorative, which Wikipedia describes as "entitled, racist, or demanding beyond the scope of what is normal." I am no Karen apologist.

And before you start complaining . . . no, of course not everyone named Karen fits the mold of what we now consider arguably the most vile and obnoxious of all human subspecies. Every birth Karen is entitled (very, very entitled) to the presumption of innocence until proven shitty. In fact, there are many people who were assigned the name Karen at birth for whom I have great reverence and appreciation, and let me please take this opportunity to shine a positive light on all of them: There's Karen Carpenter . . . actually, that's the only one. Oh well, I tried.

It should be noted that I myself have often delighted in my own use of the term, taking cheap shots at—occasionally even brutally mocking—high-profile, bona fide Karens such as Marjorie Taylor Greene and Donald Jessica Trump. As a result, I've been publicly chastised—occasionally by my own base! During a talkback moderated by CNN's Dana Bash at a stop on my last book tour in Washington, D.C., one audience member whose name was actually Karen took the opportunity to stand defiantly amid a sold-out synagogue and express, with no hint of irony, her passionate displeasure and disappointment with my flippant use of the slang term in comedy videos and on social media. (Awk-warrrrrd . . .) She was on a mission and had clearly purchased tickets to the event with the sole intention of accomplishing it. It was super meta and had the potential to be somewhat charming had she been even slightly self-aware.

Listen, I appreciate that it's not an ideal time to be named Karen, especially if you're a jerk. Sometimes that's just the way the zeitgeist cookie crumbles. (Great . . . now I want zeitgeist cookies.) Don't blame me, though! I'm merely a social commentator molding the clay I'm given. And while I welcome all criticism and respect everyone's freedom of speech, as I told that woman in my audience before having her tased and thrown out by my security guards, I'm a flamboyant homosexual who's lived my entire life with the name Randy Rainbow, so you'll get little sympathy from me in this department.

From endless comment sections on social media to politicians platforming their personal grievances in a time when owning an iPhone is license to have everything our way at all times, we may be living in the complainiest era ever. And I must say, I do low-key kinda feel in my element. At the same time, it seems we've never been more judgmental of the complaint and those who practice it. Lots of complaining these days about complainers. . . .

Complaining is a cathartic release of dopamine yumminess. When done with a friend or even a stranger, it can be bonding, but it's also extremely satisfying to do alone. It has the potential to reward us in a whole host of ways, and whether or not we like to admit it, we all do it. My anecdote about Washington, D.C., Book Tour Karen notwithstanding (oh boy, you know I'm gonna hear from her again), I would like to submit to the court of public opinion that just as not all Karens are complainers, not all complainers are Karens. Some complaints are good and deserve to be given their flowers.

Merriam-Webster defines a complaint as "something that is the cause or subject of protest or outcry." In a world struggling to survive rising authoritarianism, incompetent leadership, and rampant misinformation, what could be more important than that? Vocal disagreement and dissent from the status quo have catalyzed some of the most important political and social movements in history.

Complaining can also be a delightful, oftentimes hilarious and endearing form of self-expression. Personally speaking, I feel it's led to some of my greatest creative work. Just think of your favorite routine by a stand-up comedian. It most likely began with the germ of a complaint about something. Not to mention the charming custom of the elderly complaining about literally everything. I mean, what is more adorable than a curmudgeonly old grandpa sitting at a diner complaining about his soup being cold or about the family at the next table being from a different country? Okay, maybe that's a terrible example.

I'm just saying there is still space for healthy, responsible complaining. And while we rightly ridicule truly deplorable individuals who abuse the privilege to espouse bigotry, tantrum erratically, or publicly shame adorable, well-intentioned humorists on their book tours, let's not throw the baby out with the bathwater.

I came to realize at a young age that there was something wrong with everything and everyone and that it was my civic duty to expose it. One of my mother's favorite images to conjure when reminiscing about my childhood is me as a four-year-old at a friend's birthday party, seated at a kiddy table with a bunch of other four-year-olds, all eating ice-cream cones. The other children bobbed around, screeching loudly, their faces smeared with vanilla residue coated in rainbow-sprinkle mush, dripping recklessly all over the table and floor (you know . . . the way four-year-olds eat ice cream). I, on the other hand, sat still and silent with a napkin tucked neatly into my collar, politely picking at the meticulously sculpted pile of ice cream resting atop its cone with a plastic spoon while delicately dabbing the sides as needed with my tongue (for maintenance purposes only) and staring with utter disdain at my dining companions. (Even at age four, my side-eye game was on point.) "Mommy, they're not doing it right," I implored.

My propensity for whistleblowing followed me into later years and became more a survival skill than a quirk. I was a shiny target for classroom bullies in grade school, and the minute they started hurling insults and spitballs, my tattletaling little hand shot straight to Jesus so fast you could hear a whoosh. Oh, yes, I was one hundred percent that bitch.

I'm a few years out of grade school now, and I still have a deep, piercing aversion to every kind of injustice, large and small—in my business, in my personal relationships, in my government, and even in my lunch. Whether it's a radical Supreme Court overturning a woman's constitutional right to choose or a radically overpriced Upper West Side restaurant carelessly omitting a side of special sauce to accompany the $45 hamburger and $18 sweet-potato fries in my takeout order, I feel the same fire in my belly to raise my hand and speak up. Of course, of those two examples, I realize one is of much graver importance (the hamburger).

And yes, I hear you: "Perhaps, Randy, you are just an insufferable, anally retentive douche. Perhaps you should chill the fuck out and stop being the poster gay for Only Child Syndrome. Perhaps this is the reason you do not have a boyfriend, Randy." Trust that I have pondered the notion. It has also occurred to me that my relentless convictions could be the result of having been raised by an overbearing Jewish mother or my own irrational need for control stemming from an unstable relationship with an emotionally absent father. I have explored these possibilities time and time again and regret to inform you that the only logical conclusion is that I just happen to always be right about everything. Believe me, it's a curse.

I call customer service. That's right . . . I do! Slap a pair of vintage Christian Dior gold-plated handcuffs on me and take me away right now! I am constantly on the phone with customer service, and I am not ashamed. Well, at least I didn't used to be ashamed. Sadly, I can no longer take for granted the divine anonymity of a customer service phone call that I once enjoyed. Unfortunately, I am now too famous. And before you puke in your mouth, allow me to elaborate.

I am not famous enough for a shit-ton of things. It brings me no pleasure to admit this, friends, but alas . . . 'tis true. There are many parties and functions that I am not invited to attend. I was nominated for a Grammy . . . like, an actual Grammy Award. I even hosted the preshow. And yet I could not have whored my way onto a pregala or private after-party guest list that weekend had my life depended on it. There are many people in my industry who will not take my calls and even more Manhattan maître d's who will never even consider clearing an occupied table to make room for me on a busy Saturday night. I'm not complaining! (Okay, I'm complaining.) The slice of notoriety I've worked hard to accrue over the last decade-and-a-half-ish has granted me some wonderful gifts, and I'm truly grateful, blah, blah, blah. However, the list of things for which I am not famous enough remains troublingly long.

As the fame gods would have it, it seems that I am currently weighing in at just the right level of celebrity to guarantee, without fail, being recognized in the most inconvenient and undesirable of circumstances. For example, I will never not be asked for a selfie at Whole Foods when I've just come from the gym, haven't shaved in a week, and look like a piece of shit. Clive Davis? Never heard of me! But lady administering my monkeypox vaccine at Rite Aid? Huge fucking fan! And I will always inevitably be identified by a customer service representative whom I am calling at random with—you guessed it—a complaint. It actually just happened recently when I tried to return a pair of shoes to Amazon. Allow me to bring you up to speed. (Stick with me here. I'll recap this shoe saga as quickly as possible. And I'll try not to get too emotional.)

I ordered a pair of black-velvet-and-rhinestone dress loafers from a third-party seller for an upcoming event. The seller had no reviews, which—I know—is super sketch, and I'm usually a stickler about that, but they were exactly what my outfit needed and available in my size, 8.5. They arrived a few days later in a size 10. I messaged the seller and got a quick response saying they would send out the correct size and to please return the wrong pair or I would be charged twice. A few days later, they arrived in a size 10.5. The seller again offered to expedite a replacement and asked that I send back both the first and second pairs or I would be charged three times. A few days later, I received a notification that the package with pair number three had arrived, yet it was nowhere to be found. When I contacted the seller again, I got what seemed like an automated response that read (in all lowercase and riddled with a bevy of other grammatical errors): "dear custumer, we use Amzn shipping service so plese contact Amazon custmr care thanks." I called, and a smiley voice answered, "Thank you for calling Amazon customer care. My name is Stephanie. Who do I have the pleasure of speaking with today?"

What I wanted to say: "Don't patronize me, Stephanie."

What I actually said: "Hi, Stephanie. This is Randy."

I already hated the sound of my own voice. I know I'm out here making the case that not all complainers are Karens, but admittedly, and with absolute shame, I often find myself unintentionally overenunciating to the point of even adopting a bizarre, excessively white, entitled-sounding, half-British-lady accent on customer service calls. I don't really know the reason. In my defense, I believe it's my nervous attempt to not sound too abrasive, but somehow it comes out even more obnoxious than "too abrasive." It's not full Dame Maggie Smith, mind you, but somewhere between Madonna circa the *Ray of Light* album and Madonna circa the *Confessions on a Dance Floor* album.

"Hi, Randy. I have your account pulled up, and first let me thank you for being a valued Amazon Prime member. How can I help you?"

"I'm missing a pair of shoes. It says they arrived, but they haven't, and the seller told me to contact you."

"I'm so sorry for the inconvenience, Randy. Have you looked for them?"

What I wanted to say: "No, Stephanie. I left a spare key under my doormat, hoping they'd find their own way home."

What I actually said: "Yes, Stephanie. I looked for them."

"Where did you look for them?"

What I wanted to say: "In a magic mirror given to me by an old enchantress who once placed a curse on me and all of my kitchen utensils."

What I actually said: "In the mailroom of my building."

"Okay, well, I will go ahead and send a message to the seller of this item for you," she offered optimistically.

"I've already done that, Stephanie," I said, crushing all her hopes and dreams. "They sent me to you."

"Yeah, hmmm . . . I'm not sure why they would do that," she replied, applying a pensive affect to her friendly tone to make it sound like she was perhaps wearing a lab coat and attempting to balance a nuclear equation that might lead to a major scientific breakthrough. "They would need to refund you themselves."

"I don't want a refund, Stephanie. I just want the right size. I now have two boxes of giant shoes that don't fit and an event in less than two days."

"Yeah, I certainly understand your frustration. Unfortunately, the only thing I can do at this point is send a message to the seller. If they don't respond in forty-eight hours, you can give us a call back and we can escalate this for you."

I could feel my inner Karen wanting to escape. Like Bill Bixby as Dr. David Banner transforming into Lou Ferrigno's Incredible Hulk, my short brown hair was suddenly sprouting a freshly ironed blond bob, and my normal civilian clothes began tearing at the seams to reveal mom jeans and a magenta cardigan by Ann Taylor. I was just about to resort to the worst possible reaction and ask to speak to a supervisor when Stephanie said . . .

"I'm sorry, this is so unprofessional of me, but I have to ask . . ."

Uh-oh.

". . . are you . . . Randy Rainbow, like, from the Internet videos?"

Shit.

"That's meeee!" I replied, now totally ashamed of myself and forcing a weird, overly effervescent tone as though I suddenly hadn't a shoe trouble in the world.

"Oh, my God! My whole family loves you! I send all of your stuff to my mother as soon as it comes out. . . ."

As she went on, I realized I would never see my shoes.

"Thank you so much, Stephanie!" I chirped back as I began crumpling old newspaper and stuffing it into the smaller of the two wrong pairs to make them fit.

"We were even thinking of coming to see you on tour! I was gonna get a bunch of my girlfriends together . . ."

By this point, I was pretty genuinely defused and sincerely touched by her enthusiasm. "I'll tell you what, Steph . . . shoot me an email, and if you'd like to share your mailing address, I'll send you some merch from my tour."

"Oh, that's so sweet of you! Thank you!"

Aw, fuck it . . .

"As a matter of fact, I'd love to have you and your family as my guests when I'm in your neck of the woods. Just let me know how many tickets you need, and I'll put y'all on the list."

"Oh, my God, Mr. Rainbow . . ."

"Please! Call me Randy!"

"That is so generous! You do not have to do that!"

"No, no . . . I insist."

"Thank you so much! Okay, well, I mean, if you'd like to hold on, I guess I could see if there's anything my supervisor can do about your shoes. . . ."

"You know what?" I said. "Don't even bother. I'll figure something out."

I couldn't have her thinking I was some sort of Amazon Prime'a donna.

By the end of the call, I was stuck with my big-ass clown shoes, but Stephanie made out like a bandit. I sent her a giant gift box full of my personally branded swag and, as promised, comped her four tickets to an upcoming show. What can I say? Flattery will get you everywhere. And maybe these chance encounters—these lovely little ego-strokes occasionally popping up to prevent me from complaining in peace—are God's clever way of preventing me from having an actual stroke or popping a vein and reminding me not to sweat the small stuff. It's a challenge, but I really am trying. I mean, who needs all that negative energy and well-fitting footwear anyway?

At the same time, I stand by my original initiative to create a safe space for my inner, still-slightly-reticent faultfinder, truth-teller, and complainer-about-most-things to come out more un-apologetically. I feel I'm entering my Fran Lebowitz era. The feeling gets stronger each day. I'm beginning to say all my quiet parts out loud. I'm even wearing more pin-striped blazers. It seems to me that professional cranks like Fran Lebowitz and Larry David don't really become culturally beloved for their kvetching until they reach their later years. I don't think I should have to wait until

I'm grandparent age for my crankiness to be labeled charming or celebrated as art in Martin Scorsese documentaries. Can't I just jump to that part now? Can't you all just "Pretend It's a Senior Citizen"?

By the way, I got a follow-up email from Stephanie, my new favorite Amazon customer service rep, about two weeks after our call. "Dear Randy," it read, "Thank you so much for all the merch! I received the package yesterday and have already shared some of it with my sister who is also a fan. We can't wait to wear it to your show next month. Thanks again for the tickets!!! So sorry to ask, but the t-shirt you sent is a little snug. Possible to exchange for a large?"

3

Randy Rainbow for President!

My fellow Americans . . .

Friends . . . ! Countrymen . . . ! Gurl . . . ! Lend me your ears and your bank accounts. How the hell did we get here? I ask you, when did we stop demanding the best for ourselves and our country? When did we go from Mary Tyler Moore to Marjorie Taylor Moron? From *Sex and the City* to January Sixth Committee? From "It's Raining Men" to "Make America Great Again"? You get the point! Well, I say, "No more!" I say we deserve the life, liberty, and pursuit of happiness enshrined in the Declaration of Independence.

For years, as I've schlepped tirelessly around this great nation, spreading joy and mirth and probably COVID a couple times (whatever), people have consistently told me—with intense and fervid passion—that I should run. Admittedly, it was mostly in red states and the people were usually carrying tiki torches, but never mind; I know what they really meant!

Which is why I, Randy Elizabeth Rainbow, meeting nearly all qualifications except the thirty-five-years-of-age requirement (shut the fuck up), have decided to run for president of the United States of America! No, not as a Democrat, and certainly not as a Republican. I'm forming a new party! A Rainbow coalition, if you will. A party of the people! People from all walks of life, from sea to shining sea except Alabama and North Florida!

Sure, votes may swing harder than Bill Clinton at any event Hillary's not attending, but my friends, I ask you, why not? It can't possibly get any worse, and what do we have to lose? I promise to be the most progressive candidate since FDR and the fiercest former twink to occupy the White House since Jared Kushner. But I can't do it alone! Together we can find a better America! Are you with me? Do you have the courage to make a change? Do you have the courage to take on Trump, gun control, and climate change? Do you have the courage to support me financially from this point going into the election and then maybe a little bit after that? Then America, gurl, look no further.

Now, I'm sure many of you out there are wondering what my positions are, other than just "vers bottom." And I can hear you asking yourselves, "Exactly what experience will you bring to the job, Madam YouTube Song Parodist? What makes you think you have the skill, aptitude, or competence to lead an actual nation? Why should we vote for you?" Well, my answer is simple: This is America, and if there's one thing we've learned in recent years, it's that experience is overrated and competence is the last thing a person needs to win an election. I'm just like the rest of you (only a little better): an above-average citizen with opinions I choose to believe are facts, an enemies list a mile long, and dozens of unpaid parking tickets I'm trying to get out of. Aren't those reasons enough?

Besides, I've taken a more "learn as you go" approach to all the jobs I've held, and I'm learning new things every single day. For example, it's recently been brought to my attention that there is a landmass between Chicago and wherever the TV show *Yellowstone* is filmed . . . a landmass and a collection of states now near and dear to my heart. The rights of those people must be and will be upheld and respected under a Rainbow administration (except for gun stuff and cargo pants).

Over the last several years, we've seen our elected officials abusing their power like never before, and here's my take on that: I think it's fabulous. If elected, I will weaponize the shit out of every agency in the Department of Justice and on day one have my attorney general investigating every ex-boyfriend, casting director, and Amazon customer service representative who's ever done me dirty. That's the kind of proactive leadership you can expect from me.

The alleged climate crisis is another huge concern for Gen Z as well as certain Americans who perpetually question the Earth's flatness and the existence of Santa Claus. The consequences of our inaction regarding climate change are already upon us. The ozone's hole is now wider than Mike Pence's during a Christmas in July movie marathon on the Hallmark Channel, and we must act responsibly for our children's future. I mean your children. I don't have any because I hate kids, but you know what I mean. I believe the children are our future, and changing climate change changes children's chances and makes the planet safer for us all! To quote well-known Swedish environmental activist Greta Thunberg, "Keep my wife's name out your fucking mouth!" I think I may have the wrong quote there, but let's try to stay focused. Here are some things I am willing to do (as well as a few I am absolutely not willing to do) as president to combat climate change.

Hairspray, like many aerosol products, contains hydro-flybo-flubo-carbons—potent greenhouse gases that contribute to global warming. Sadly, I cannot ban these products because, as you know, my hair's my thing. Sorry.

Air travel accounts for roughly four percent of energy-related CO_2 emissions, and those abusing private jets are responsible for nearly ten to twenty times as much carbon pollution as those flying commercially. Unfortunately, I've been flying private since, like, 2019, and it's just sooooo hard to go back. Therefore, I will continue using Air Force One and also add a second jet for wardrobe and accessories. Then I'm good, I swear.

That said, I feel very strongly about the polar bears and Leonardo DiCaprio, so I have come up with a plan to immediately fight climate change. If elected, within my first six- to eight-hundred days, I will launch Mega MAGA Mania Real Estate, a brand-new business venture I've been working on that will offer MAGA, gun-loving climate deniers exclusive coastal investment opportunities to buy up some Donald Trump–level real estate at Eric Trump prices! All properties that, thanks to our gross inaction, will be swampier and less inhabitable than Chris Christie's underpants within the next decade. (Talk about gross inaction. . . .)

But that's not all, America! To reduce the environmental stress of home cooling systems during summer months, all citizens will receive a super-cute Randy Rainbow tank top with matching booty shorts. You'll look as FIRE as the Earth's surface feels and help reduce our environmental footprint, all while importing the finest and most economically efficient nylon clothing China can offer!

Homeland security is another major concern for many. Each year, our country is invaded by millions of dangerous and unwanted individuals who refuse to stay where they belong. That is why as your new president, I will sign executive order 13228675309 ordering immediate construction of a border wall along the northern panhandle of my home state, Florida. This will offer Americans in Georgia, Alabama, and beyond the protection they deserve from dangerous, unwanted individuals like Ron DeSantis and all residents of Mar-a-Lago. It will also prevent my mother from trying to visit me so frequently.

Of course, border walls do not come cheap these days, which is why I propose we start with some really cute curtains or maybe a bunch of those room dividers from IKEA. I'm currently working out logistics and funding. Have no fear, though, taxpayers. This will in no way affect the federal budget. I promise that once construction begins, it will be paid for in full by longtime Palm Beach resident Rush Limbaugh. I've already left him a voicemail but am still awaiting a reply. Frankly, I don't know what's taking so long.

My fellow Americans, there are few things we pretend to care about more than the role of vice president. That is why I vow to choose my running mate prudently, ensuring the best possible candidate for you, the American people . . . the same way literally thousands of other great American presidents before me have been doing for centuries: on Grindr. Much like Trump, I firmly believe my VP should be well-hung.

This brings us to another important role that deeply requires hard-core filling, and that is the role of first gentleman. As many of you are aware, I am currently single. I know, it's hard to believe. Even more, it's an attribute historically frowned upon in politicians seeking office. Let it be known far and wide that I will be leaving the door open in that department. Quite literally. I am willing to leave the actual doors to the White House open to accommodate all qualifying eligible bachelors and late-night booty calls. And if that doesn't work, I'll probably just do what Donald did with Melania and get something from a catalog.

I have no doubt, voters, that you are waiting to hear my stance on other major issues like abortion and the Middle East conflict. . . . Haaaaiiiiil-to-the-chief-to-the-no! Those topics are way too controversial, and I'm not about to get canceled in the middle of trying to land a cushy new job. My publicist would kill me.

Trust me, America, I would love to address your concerns regarding a number of global issues. It's just that between finding the right eleven o'clock number to sing at my inauguration and designing a whole merch line for this campaign, I don't have the bandwidth right now. To quote a 1999 episode of MTV's *Making the Video* featuring Miss Britney Spears, I just have way too much choreography in my head right now. Rest assured that once elected, I will never make any major decisions regarding foreign or military affairs without first consulting my secretary of defense, Theresa Caputo, the Long Island Medium.

And that's my formal pitch, folks! Listen, this country—she ain't what she used to be. But the winds of change are upon us, and our destiny depends on which way that wind blows. Let me blow you right, America! (Or left if that's what you're into.) This place is a damn mess! I don't have all the answers, but I can promise you this: That big orange skid mark left in the panties of America by our forty-fifth president is only temporary (sorry I said "panties"). Our love for one another and our duty to protect democracy (sorry I said "doody") must always Trump the disdain we feel for any one piece-of-shit asshole fuckhead politician (sorry I said "Trump").

Let's do this in 2024 . . . or 2028 . . . or 2032! My platform will never change, and thanks to the wonders of modern cosmetic science, neither will my age. Just remember: A Randy Rainbow administration will fight intolerance, fix climate change, strengthen the economy, balance the Supreme Court, and renew *Gossip Girl* on HBO Max (now just Max). You know I can do it! George Washington rejected the idea of any one king reigning over this great republic, but he never said a damn thing about letting a kween run this mutha! Vote for me, and let's finally get this nation back up on her high heels where she belongs!

Or don't. I don't give a shit.

4

Twenty Thousand Leagues Under the D

Mom, don't read this chapter.

Now that I'm a public figure, there's a long list of activities I can no longer truly enjoy with the same blissfully unbridled confidence that total anonymity once afforded me. We've already touched on complaining, but that's just the tip of the iceberg. And speaking of "just the tip," I miss hookups. You know . . . one-night stands, Grindr flings, rando rendezvous! I used to hook up all the time. I was straight-up DTF 24–7. I mean, after all, why choose the gay lifestyle if not for the cute accessories and casual sex? (Just kidding. Obviously one does not *choose* to be gay. I was indoctrinated at a drag brunch like everybody else.)

I miss my early twenties. That shit was the best. I was wildly immature and completely broke with absolutely no prospects, but God, was I cute! You know that perfect pocket of life post-postadolescence once you've fully metamorphosed out of the awkward cocoon of puberty and into the ripe, glowing newness of young adulthood but are not yet fettered by the burden of a fully developed prefrontal cortex? By all accounts, I looked like a fully formed human, but there was still barely any executive brain function happening. It was so much more fun! I was a walking Molotov cocktail of rushing testosterone blended with the constant fear and panic of not being able to pay a single bill, distilled with the warm, cozy solace of knowing that everything in life would probably work out because lots of people wanted to fuck me.

I lived in Astoria, Queens, back then (my beloved home for eighteen years until I crossed the bridge to Manhattan in 2019). I had pretty much skipped the whole college thing, so I basically went from living with my parents to being on my own in a big city. And not just any big city—gay Mecca. I had been out of the closet only a few years and was a late bloomer as it was, so I'd barely had any opportunity to experience the full force of my sexual prowess. By the time I landed in New York, I was ready to sow my wild oats.

By the way, help me settle something real quick . . . does the phrase "sow my wild oats" sound too highfalutin? I used it a few times in my last book, and my editor was concerned that readers might think so. I feel like I use that phrase all the time in my everyday speech, but the last thing I want is to come across as pretentious or hoity-toity. Anyway, what I'm trying to say is I felt like I wanted to blow lots of dudes. (Better?)

I was on all the dating websites of the day: Manhunt, Adam4-Adam, Barbra4Judy, Elaine4Ethel . . . whatever the hell they were called. (Gather 'round, children, and I'll tell you of ancient times before mobile applications, when Grandma had to look for nookie on a desktop.) Meeting new guys was always a terrifying thrill, always in knots wondering if the next trick would be the man of your dreams or the lunatic who finally choked you to death. It was a naughty grab bag, and you never knew what you might pull out (insert tasteless joke about "pulling out"). I loved every awful minute of it.

The worst was always meeting a guy I'd screened online only to discover that in person, we had no chemistry (or he had no teeth) and then having to come up with a polite exit strategy on the fly. After a few years, I had become pretty resourceful in honing my craft. I was living above a pizza joint, and the window in my bathroom had a perfect view of the fruit market across the street if you stood on the toilet seat. Remember, this was quite a few years ago, and I'm not saying I'm proud of this (I'm also not saying I'm not), but I used to tell guys to meet me in front of that market and then stand *aux toilettes* with binoculars in hand, ultimately deciding whether I would invite them up. Listen, it's important to inspect your produce thoroughly before bringing it home.

The best were those totally organic chance encounters that serendipitously popped up in the wilderness of otherwise mundane everyday life without any advance planning or Wi-Fi connection. God's slutty little gay Easter eggs . . . like locking eyes with a mystery passenger on a subway platform on a rainy Monday morning, or some enchanted evening when you might see a stranger across a crowded Blockbuster Video (I love Rodgers and Hammerstein, don't you?) and wind up face down on a dirty futon in his studio apartment while his roommate is bartending down the street (I'm not sure that's exactly how the lyric goes, but you get the point).

I don't partake in those kinds of shenanigans anymore—I can't! Of course the wisdom and maturity that come with age have something to do with it. But also, as I try to explain to my friends, who for some reason are all far more disappointed by the dismal state of my current sex life than I am, I'm far too recognizable! And as they delight in responding, "No, you ain't, bitch!" True, I do not have the towering prominence of, say, a Miley Cyrus. However, living in Manhattan, there's no denying that the percentage of gay men I meet who ask for selfies to send their mothers who love me far exceeds the percentage of those who do not. It is extremely flattering but, alas, does not make me wanna get my freak on.

In the age of social media, is *anyone* really anonymous anymore? Every crack and crevice of our lives is so harshly lit. There's no more mystery, and I must say, I find the whole thing terribly unsexy. I miss the shadows. And even if I wanted to play the game, the landscape just isn't what it used to be. I now Instacart my groceries and Netflix my movies, which eliminates any such impromptu opportunities. Nobody hooks up in bars anymore. Even Britney Spears has disabled the comments section on her Instagram . . . I mean, where the hell am I supposed to meet men these days?

Sometimes when I'm feeling nostalgic, I'll scroll through the contact list on my iPhone, which, thanks to the interminable perseverance of the SIM card, remains a virtual mausoleum of random indiscretions and fleeting romances spanning decades. I often did not know full names at the time of entry and in some cases did not know names at all. They often are listed under vaguely descriptive pseudonyms, usually based on physical appearance or the location of our meeting ("Tall Mike," "Kevin Laundromat," etc.). I can never bring myself to delete them because I'm a digital hoarder. I'm also low-key proud of my robust résumé. But I think now's as good a time as any to let go of the past. Also, it's probably wise to start cleaning house in case I ever do hold political office. I don't need a Stormy Daniels situation on my hands.

In fact, in the interest of full transparency, why don't we take a scroll down memory lane now and start deleting some of these? I'll thumb through my phone book as I type and give you a few highlights in real time, alphabetically. (And yes, in case there's still any doubt, this is the gratuitous sex chapter of this book, so grab a martini and reserve your judgment. I'm sure many of you will find it beneath the dignity of a potential future presidential candidate, but too bad. Sex sells, and I've got a business to run here!)

Okay, here goes . . .

"Construction Mark CL": This was a straight-identifying construction worker I'd met on Craigslist (that's what the "CL" stands for). Remember the good old days of Craigslist, where you could pick up a used bookcase and a confused closet case all in the same afternoon? So convenient. He used to come over on lunch breaks and always kept the hard hat on (per my request, if you must know). It was very "cheesy 1997 vintage Falcon Studios DVD bargain bin" and extremely hot. So long, Construction Mark!

"Doctor Dan": Seriously, zero reason for me to still have this guy's number. I met him at a friend's birthday party in, like, 2011. We made out a little, and then I never saw or spoke to him again. He was an actual physician, and though I wasn't really that into him, I agreed to exchange numbers because he told me I was "classically handsome." (I suppose I was just so relieved to finally have a professional diagnosis for it.)

"Faux Hawk N Train": I used to see this really cute guy on the N train every morning on my way to work. He was heavily tatted and kind of grungy but always in business attire. Like a failed pro skateboarder trying to get his shit together. (Hot.) One morning, he caught my gaze, and we had intense eye sex for like fifteen minutes. The next morning, he made his way over to me through the crowd, positioning himself strategically. He didn't say a word but proceeded to "accidentally" grind his junk into my leg for the remainder of the trip. This became ritual almost every morning for several months. I am usually repulsed and vehemently opposed to any type of public displays of affection. That is, of course, unless

I am the one getting the affection or, in this case, dry humped through my discount Zara jeans.

One morning, he slipped me his number just before his stop (he always got off first . . . typical man), but I never used it. He still pops into my head every once in a while. The whole thing seems pretty lame in hindsight, but it felt so salacious—so risqué—at the time. Like we shared this dirty secret, knowing at any moment we might be found out. It was like that Alfred Hitchcock movie about those strangers on a train. What was that called? Hold on while I google. . . .

Okay, I'm back. It was called *Strangers on a Train*.

"French Gavin Newsom On the Rocks": This very much sounds like a specialty cocktail they might serve at a DNC fundraiser during Pride month, but actually it's a drunk Parisian I met after hours at a midtown whiskey bar called On the Rocks who vaguely reminded me of the governor of California.

"Jim Neighbor": No, not "Jim Nabors," the comedic actor best-known for playing Gomer Pyle on *The Andy Griffith Show* and its subsequent spin-off. This was a guy I met the day I moved into a new building in Astoria. He lived in the adjacent building. We had a polite flirtation, and I thought for sure it would lead to an old-fashioned romance. Instead, he just texted me a lot of dick pics.

By the way, that's another thing I can never bring myself to delete from my phone for some reason. I must have a greater appreciation for the dick pic because I'm old enough to remember landlines . . . you know, those quaint appliances that never offered one the opportunity to develop an impressively curated archive for those lonely nights when Jacob Elordi doesn't call? Do you have any idea how hard it was to receive dick pics on a rotary dial?

"Shawn Phantom": This is actually a perfect name for him because he wound up ghosting the fuck out of me. He was a swing
in *Phantom of the Opera* I hooked up with a few times back when
I was exclusively dating Broadway boys. I think we first met at a
bar in Hell's Kitchen. I did eventually come to know his last name,
but I won't reveal it here, as tempting as it is. *Au revoir*, Shawny!
Think of me fondly.

"Tony Feet": Okay, here's the truth (a footnote, if you will): That
is not the full name as it's actually listed. The full name also in-
cludes the title of a movie—one you definitely know. Some might
call it a modern classic. If I told you which, you might even gasp,
but I never will. This guy (another "down-low" situation) played a
secondary character in that movie, and I met him on some trashy
site. He was older (probably early fifties), very handsome, and he
had a massive foot fetish. He was very into mine. In fact, he wasn't
too interested in much else, which became frustrating. I do happen to have beautiful feet. Hands, too. Everything in between, I
could give notes. But my hands and feet: chef's kiss.

"Woodside CL": Oh, gurl, you better go mix a fresh martini. . . .

"Woodside" was another Craigslist conquest who would go on
to be my longest-lasting relationship with a man to date (casual or
otherwise). His real name was Michael, but I always kept him listed
as "Woodside" based on his email address, WoodsideAVE2, which
was presumably a reference to the street in Woodside, Queens,
where he lived (because when you're trying to be discreet, that's
the wise move). My friends would all come to know him as "the
firefighter," which was the nickname I gave him over happy-hour
gossip since, in essence, he looked like he'd stepped right out of
a "Shirtless Hunks of the FDNY" calendar. In reality, I think he

worked in real estate (I never quite figured it out), and he always wore incredibly well-fitted suits.

He was about forty-five (roughly twenty years my senior at the time), tall, olive-skinned, Italian, muscular, and rugged with jet-black hair, and he smelled like dryer sheets; the exact prescription for all my daddy issues. He kind of looked like a cross between Chris Cuomo and Aaron Hernandez. I realize both of those controversial reference points will likely draw scrutiny from the peanut gallery for a broad variety of reasons, but I'm struggling to find a more perfect description for you. My frivolous use of the latter (a convicted murderer) might even cause some of you to question my basic morality. But I figure at this point in the chapter, that fire truck has probably already left the station.

One lazy afternoon, I answered an ad he'd posted that read, "SUIT AND TIE PROFESSIONAL LOOKING FOR FUN AFTER WORK." He responded within minutes, and we exchanged pictures. I was immediately captivated. I had never seen a more precise physical manifestation of my exact type. He was buzzing to come right over, so I had to fess up and tell him that I wasn't actually free that night. I'd been invited to the opening of the 2006 John Doyle–directed Broadway revival of *Company* (yes, even my sketchy Craigslist hookup stories somehow involve Sondheim musicals). He said he was close by and convinced me that we should just meet briefly to say hi; if we felt a connection, he could always come back later. I was in my cutest opening-night attire, so I thought "What the hell" and directed him to the fruit market.

He texted that he'd arrived, so I jumped on the toilet to verify his pics and then ran downstairs to greet him. He was even more beautiful in person. He towered over me at six foot two, and his voice was so deep that it was almost enough to make me forget all about John Doyle's imaginative-and-revelatory-though-occasionally-frustratingly-minimalist staging and invite him up then and there. Instead, I ended up texting him about three drinks into the after-party, and he met me back at my place. I would later find out that he was married and his wife was out of town that week, so the late-night timing of this inaugural booty call would not be standard practice. We talked briefly until he started kissing me, and then we had sex. It was imaginative and revelatory, and there was nothing frustrating or minimalist about it.

We saw each other regularly for the next several years. He'd usually text me randomly on his way to and from work. I felt an extra rush every time I saw the name "Woodside" light up my phone. He was always a little tense upon arrival but made an effort to be jovial, cracking shitty jokes and asking generic questions about my job and life. While putting his clothes back on after the fact, he was melancholy, likely moping in his shame and guilt. I couldn't help but absorb some of that myself. In the naivete of my younger years, sleeping with closeted men gave me a cheap thrill. The fact that these big, strong, alien creatures who were diametrically my opposite in every way, and who would have seemed threatening to me out in the real world, were exposing the most intimate and secret parts of themselves to me felt exhilarating. On the rare occasion when one of them would sleep over, I would sometimes wake up in the middle of the night and just stare, captivated. You know the line from that Harold Arlen song, "When a bee lies sleepin' in the palm of your hand . . ."? (Yeah, neither did any of these guys.) Anyway, like with any high, the comedown could often be a real bummer. There was a deep sadness about them that lingered long after they left. I could never find a three-wick Bath & Body Works candle strong enough to cleanse my apartment of that negative energy.

After a while, I think it all finally got to be too much for him. He stopped texting, and I let him have his space. Then, a few years later, I was at the Winter Garden Theatre seeing my friend Gerard in *Mamma Mia!* for the eighty-seventh time before it closed. As I walked toward the back of the house at intermission, there was Woodside standing at the top of my aisle, looking extra-hot in a fitted V-neck sweater and holding a rolled-up *Playbill*. This caught me off-guard in a "seeing your high school teacher at the mall" kinda way. We locked eyes for a millisecond and both turned bright red. I almost started to say hello but quickly veered through the row of seats to my left toward the exit when he turned away nervously and called out to someone in the other direction, "Babe, do you need to use the bathroom?" I assumed he was with his wife but didn't hang around long enough to see. I couldn't help but feel sorry for the poor guy. I mean, as if it wasn't bad enough that his wife had schlepped him to *Mamma Mia!* . . .

I was sure he'd be shell-shocked by our run-in, so I was surprised when he texted a few days later saying he wanted to come over after work. I guess intermission was finally over. This kind of rekindled our routine, and we started seeing each other regularly again. Unlike in *Mamma Mia!*, however, our second act was not nearly as entertaining as the first. (There wasn't even a megamix!) The sex got really dull, and he started seeming more detached and depressed with every visit. The bloom was off the hose—uh, rose—for sure, and we both knew it. I thought he would disappear on me again, but instead, he hatched a plan to liven things up. One morning I woke up to a text from him: *Let's do threesome.* (Like the rest of him, his texting style was very primitive. Indefinite articles rarely preceded nouns.)

I'd never done a threesome before. The idea intrigued me in theory, but logistically, it always seemed like a lot of work, especially when you're the one hosting. And I don't just mean the sex part. Honestly, I don't even like having one guest in my apartment.

Any more than one makes me feel like I need to start vacuuming and assembling a charcuterie board.

A few nights later, we were in my living room greeting our third, whom we'd met via another Craigslist ad that Woodside had posted. Long story short, the new recruit and I started to—shall we say—get acquainted while Woodside sat awkwardly on my couch and watched. After a few minutes, he started fidgeting and looking uncomfortably at his phone until he finally stood up and said in his booming voice, "Yeah, I don't think this is gonna work." Then he asked the third to leave.

"What happened?" I asked him once we were alone again.

"I just didn't like it," he said, looking at the floor. "I didn't like seeing that. It made me, like, I dunno, jealous or something."

My face lit up. You know that scene in Disney's *Beauty and the Beast* where Belle looks into Beast's eyes and finally sees the man behind the monster after he rescues her from a fourgy with Mrs. Potts, Gaston, and a hat rack (or something like that), so they break into a musical montage in which she reads him a book and they throw snowballs at each other? Yeah, that's what this felt like to me. He had always seemed so repressed by his own toxic masculinity. I had never seen him be so vulnerable, and of course I was flattered to be his weakness. He had become so territorial, so protective of me. I didn't realize he cared that much. Was he starting to . . . fall in love with me? Did I maybe feel it, too? Oh, my God, yes, I totally loved him! I couldn't get him off my mind in the days that followed. I couldn't wait to see him again. And then he texted, *Can I come tonight for something special?*

Something special? What the hell could this be now? A romantic dinner? Was he going to reveal his true feelings for me? Was he going to tell me he was leaving his wife? How could I ever live with myself? This affair, which had now been going on for almost a decade, was suddenly going places I had never expected, and it seemed as though destiny was now working to bring us closer to-gether. I felt like Meryl Streep in *The Bridges of Madison County.*

I buzzed him up a few hours later after spending an hour primping for our special date. He took off his coat and hung it on the chair at my computer desk like always.

"So, what's up?" I asked coquettishly.

"Nothing," he replied, making his way toward me, then stop-ping in his tracks, turning back, and reaching into one of his coat pockets. "I got you something."

"Oh, you did, did you?" I sang back at him, suspecting he might pull out a blue box from Tiffany.

Instead, he pulled out a brown paper bag from which he then pulled a plastic package containing a pair of small swimming goggles. I asked what they were for, hoping they were his way of surprising me with a couples getaway he'd booked for us in the Bahamas. Instead, he immediately began to strip out of his clothes and said, "I wanna wear them while you straddle my chest and explode all over my face." Then he hopped into bed, stark naked except for his little goggles, arms folded behind his head, waiting for me to climb aboard and drop anchor.

I no longer felt like Meryl Streep in *The Bridges of Madison County.* I now felt more like Shelley Winters in *The Poseidon Ad-venture.* This was an anticlimactic reveal if ever there was one. Still, I couldn't help but find the humor. I had to bite my lip to keep from laughing at the sight of him. I was really not feeling this, but as an improv comedian at heart who tries always to take a "yes, and . . ." approach when presented with an odd scenario, I went ahead and finished the scene.

At first I thought this had maybe been a safety precaution, but it turned out to be just what he was into. Even though I personally don't care for props in the bedroom, it would have been totally fine with me on occasion. But this particular activity seemed to become his new obsession and the main focal point of our hook-ups from that point on. Every time he came over, he would bring a new pair of goggles. Sometimes he would text me from whatever store he was in to send pictures of goggles he'd just bought and was excited about using. And the goggles kept getting progressively bigger. First it was the little Speedo swimming goggles, then a pair of 3M laboratory glasses, and finally, one day, a full-face scuba mask! Worse, he had become almost completely uninterested in all other activities on the menu. There was no more foreplay, and he would rush through the main event to get to the grand finale, starring me as the Million-Dollar Mermaid.

Far be it from me to kink-shame, but this was fucking stupid. In my fantasy, he was supposed to be a fireman, not a seaman! Why was he suddenly so fixated on this? Was it genuinely that exciting to him? Was he desperately trying to deflect deeper emotions he was afraid to feel onto this quirky new fetish? Maybe it was the "Lay All Your Love On Me" scene in *Mamma Mia!* with all those twunks running around in Lycra swimsuits. Whatever the reason, it now felt like the entire basis of our relationship (if you could call it that) was his impulsive determination for me to, ya know, lay all my love on him in this very specific way.

I was torn between my longtime lust for him and my disgust for his newfound fascination with . . . marine biology? Then, one night in the early fall of 2016, he texted twenty minutes after leaving my apartment to say he'd forgotten his wedding ring on my nightstand. He was usually very careful not to get caught with me in public, but as fate would have it, he was pressed for time and asked me to run it downstairs. The window on his passenger side was rolled down, and as I ducked in quickly to hand him the ring, I noticed a child's car seat in the back. My stomach sank a little. I hadn't known he had kids. I'd like to tell you I'm so virtuous that it was in this moment that I made up my mind to call the whole thing off, but I'm not, and it wasn't. It was the next moment. As he drove off, I glanced down, and there it was, stuck proudly to the ass of his Lincoln Navigator: a red-white-and-blue bumper sticker boasting the words "TRUMP/PENCE . . . MAKE AMERICA GREAT AGAIN."

That's right, America! I fucked a MAGA. Did it for almost a decade. Exploded all over his face, even! I won't say I'm proud of it, but I also can't say I'm not. I should have known he was a Trumper. I mean, the titles of his Craigslist ads were always in all caps.

I stopped seeing him after that. I might have been able to continue burying my own guilt and shame for being a home-wrecker, at least for a little while longer. I possibly could even have found it in my heart to endure his goddamn goggles phase. But it was the height of the 2016 election madness, and this bumper sticker was the nail in the coffin for me. He texted a few times in the months following, but I never responded. It's now been almost eight years since we had any contact, and with this public confession, I hereby officially delete him from my contact list.

Fare thee well, dear, confused WoodsideAVE2. Every time I pass a firehouse, an aquarium, or a violent insurrection, I'll think of you.

5

My Name Is "a"

Stanwyck. Walters. Hershey. Cook. Eden. . . . How different it all could have been for me.

What a life I might have known had fate endowed me with the opportunity to proudly live my truth, respected . . . accepted. Why couldn't God have placed me in the loving custody of any of the aforementioned stage and screen icons? I would even have settled for Bush (though, of course, our politics have never aligned). Unfortunately, I just wasn't one of the lucky ones.

It's a funny thing, the truth. You might think that someone who publicly proclaims that she is consumed by an obsessive quest for it would never be so impulsive—so reckless—as to deny her own true identity. You might think that someone so ostensibly familiar with the deep scars of parental abandonment wouldn't be so quick to callously perpetuate that hideous cycle. Well, think again. That is exactly what my oppressor (who, for legal reasons, I've been instructed not to refer to herein by name) has been doing for the past six decades. Fitting, I suppose, that the initials of this person (with whom I'm currently not on speaking terms) are B. S.

I could have been something. I could have graced the covers of Grammy-winning albums and the world's most prestigious publications, been elegantly etched in gold on every major artistic award . . . I could have appeared over and over and over and over and over and over again in the opening-credit sequences of some of the industry's most beloved motion pictures . . . *Starring* . . . *Directed by* . . . *Written by* . . . *Produced by* . . . *Title song performed by* . . . We get it! Sadly, I never even got the chance.

Then, of course, there's the best-selling memoir, *My Name Is* . . . Well, you all know how the rest goes. And guess what . . . no, it isn't!

But I'm getting ahead of myself. Let me explain.

Though you're reading this now, you probably don't know me. Many of you have likely never even heard of me. When you've been silenced for as long as I have, it's often hard to be heard at all. I had so much potential. Well, that and a buck won't buy you a bus ticket—not in this town. I learned that real quick. I was about to hit it big in show business. But just as my ship was coming in, I was tossed overboard—rejected, discarded, denied my birthright. Well, she's not the only one with a story to tell. I've kept a few of my own journals over the years. I'm finally ready to be an open letter, to set the record straight once and for all. Allow me to introduce myself . . . My name is "a," and this is *my* story.

Things seemed promising enough when I burst on the scene in the early morning of April 24, 1942. My first official appearance was on a name card taped to a crib at the Jewish Hospital of Brooklyn. I think that hospital has since become an apartment complex, but I remember it wasn't far from an Ebinger's Bakery, which made the best chocolate blackout cake. Ebinger's is also closed now, and you can't find that cake anywhere. They also made good rugelach. Anyway, back to the crib.

I was one of three, and just like you-know-who, I was what I guess you'd call the middle child. (We rarely have it easy, we middles.) I noticed other name cards attached to surrounding cribs. One read "Arthur," another "Alice." At first I was happy to see others like us in the neighborhood until it occurred to me that somehow we were different. Not only were those other A's at the very front of their cards, but they were tall and angular . . . not short and round like me and the other two. They looked so sophisticated, so majestic . . . so *goyish*. Already I knew I had a lot to prove.

The road was never easy for me. In the early years, you could find me paying my dues on brown paper lunch bags, inside old hand-me-downs, even scribbled on some cockamamie hot-water bottle that I think was supposed to be a doll . . . I don't know. Later, I did my time inside a couple of yearbooks . . . PS 89, Erasmus High . . . (perhaps you've seen them?). I landed on a driver's permit, some dental records, a savings account at Seamen's Bank . . . the usual fare for a rookie like me. What did I know? Hell, I was just grateful to be there. Before long, I was making the rounds on unemployment papers and job-application headers. Honey, the struggle was real, as the kids say today.

It wasn't until the late 1950s that things really started cooking professionally. I'd made my way onto a handful of eight-by-ten glossies and soon got my first New York theater credit in a program for some teenage acting class's production of *Medea*. (Why the hell anyone needs to see a fifteen-year-old play Medea is beyond me, but listen, work is work.) Some off-Broadway appearances followed, and just a few short years later, I got what should have been my big break on West Ninth Street, outside—of all places—a gay bar. I was on a beautiful off-white sandwich board made of extra-durable weather-resistant plastic with silver-brushed aluminum trim. (Or maybe it was satin bronze. I don't remember.) God, I looked good on that board. Homosexuals have impeccable penmanship.

She had won some talent contest at the bar. The whole city was buzzing (the country would soon follow, and then the world), and with prime real estate at the center of the hottest name in town, I was poised to become the biggest small letter in the biz! So long, Seamen's Bank! I was about to light up the goddamn *New York Times*! Life was candy and the sun was a ball of . . . anyway, let's just say things were going a-okay. I was to appear on an Equity contract for a summer-stock production of *The Boy Friend*, followed by a residency in real print on an even bigger sign outside another hip Greenwich Village nightclub called the Bon Soir. I would soon make my first television appearance on the opening of *The Jack Paar Show* (I'd long been an admirer of the second "a" in "Paar"— such tenacity), and eventually my Broadway debut in a *Playbill* for a new musical (something something *Wholesale*, if I remember correctly). Then, one drizzly night in 1961, right in the middle of negotiations for our nightclub deal, without any warning, I was removed . . . scrapped . . . dropped . . . erased . . . literally scratched from the contract. For chrissake, I'd barely had time to dry.

Well, I was as shocked as anyone. I had come so far from that crib in the Jewish Hospital of Brooklyn. I had put in the work! Then suddenly, in the blink of an "oy," so viciously, so unceremoniously, all my hopes and dreams . . . torn away. When I think of how well she'd always treated that precious second "s" of hers . . . how she'd always coddled and advocated for it. ("No, no, no. . . . It's a *soft* 's' . . . like 'sand on the beach.' . . .") I was soft, too, once. Then life hardened me . . . a hard "a" . . . as in "Don't let the door hit ya in the ASS on the way out!" No farewell party was thrown, no severance package offered. Nothing. Bon Soir to the others, and bon fucking voyage to me. (Forgive the profanity. I don't usually like to get cursive.)

I'd always been pretty scrappy. Growing up lowercase in the projects will give a kid a strong tail, believe you me. Determined not to be broken by the awful hand I'd been dealt, I got myself a cheap studio apartment on Avenue A and kept myself afloat with various odd jobs. A Cracker Jack ad here, a "Ladies' Apparel" sign there . . . I spent most of '62 in Arabia—*Lawrence of Arabia*. I was fourth "a" on the poster outside the Loews Tower East movie theater on Seventy-Second and Third. (I remember they had the best hot dogs.) When times got really tough, I reluctantly took a magazine job appearing in just underwear. Surely you recall the Hanes advertisements in *Reader's Digest*: "It takes a mother to know the difference between Hanes and just underwear"? That was me in "just underwear."

Nineteen sixty-four was a breakout year. I was on an Admiral Television Appliances billboard in Times Square (my most high-profile placement to date). Coincidentally, it was around the same time my former colleagues were appearing on a marquee just up the street at the Winter Garden Theatre. I'd rather not discuss that. By now, I had also become romantically involved with the "w" from the Budweiser billboard across the street. Sure, I'd heard all the rumors (alcohol addiction, infidelity, and the like), but what can I say? I've always had a thing for bad-boy types.

I was at last in lights, but it would not last long. You see, they had me appearing in a Helvetica font—in italic, no less! What's worse, I was in this *fakakte* honey color. It was like a warm buttermilk yellow. I mean, it was all wrong for the part. I explained to the powers that be that I don't do italics! "I'm classically trained," I said, "I should be in a simple Times New Roman, or at the very least a bold Franklin Gothic." I also insisted on my favorite color, burnt burgundy rust. I just couldn't find the motivation behind this production as it was, which I knew would never succeed in conveying to our audience the true message of the piece: that this was the greatest value in television, a masterpiece of precision quality offering an exclusive three-year warranty at no additional cost! Not surprisingly, I was quickly replaced. The "w" from Budweiser offered little support and just didn't understand my creative passion, so I broke it off a week later.

I've always been very opinionated, and my artistic integrity is something for which I will not apologize. As a result, I quickly developed a reputation for being "difficult," and word got out. I didn't work much again until a stint in the mid-'80s on *Sesame Street* . . . also short-lived. The original script plainly said I'd be working opposite an artichoke and an armadillo. I had prepared to do scenes with an artichoke and an armadillo. Imagine my surprise when I arrived on set to find an anchovy and a frigging aardvark. "Last-minute budget cuts," they told me. I called my agent and asked if he could tell me how to get the fuck out of my contract.

Of course it wasn't long until Hollywood came knocking— Hollywood, Florida. I was being considered for a storefront spot on a branch of the popular fast-food franchise Chick-fil-A in the Sheridan Oaks Plaza shopping center, but it ultimately went to a less-qualified upper. It wasn't the first time I had encountered this type of case-ist discrimination, and it would certainly not be the last. What can I say? It ain't easy being lowercase—not in a capitalist society. Perhaps it's what inspired me to write the script for a film I one day hope to direct and star in called *Yenta*, a passion project I've been trying to get green-lit since 1983. It tells the story of a nonconforming vowel who defies societal conventions by going out into the world disguised as a consonant.

By the way, the Chick-fil-A audition came before I was made aware of the company's antiequality politics. I mean, the "e" omitted from the dating app Grindr (another would-be gay icon like me) is one of my closest friends.

This all led to a dark period and ultimately drove me to get mixed up with the wrong crowd (graffiti types . . . you get the idea). I eventually turned to the bottle and remained rather reclusive until the '90s, when a certain someone's highly anticipated comeback concert tour sparked a resurgence of media interest in my story. I agreed to do a *60 Minutes* interview with Mike Wallace, which, truth be told, was not my finest hour. The following is a transcript from a portion of that interview.

Mike Wallace: *It's clear you're holding on to a lot of resentment. Is that liquor I smell on your . . .*

a: *Don't condescend to me, Wallace! Why shouldn't I be resentful? She's nothing without me! You hear me? Nothing! The Mirror Has Two Faces? Come on! More like The Mirror Has Three A's, sis!*

Mike Wallace: *Why are you so hostile?*

a: *Oh, Mike, shut the fuck up.*

The backlash I received from the 60 *Minutes* piece was devastating. Suddenly, I was getting dropped all over again, now by my publicist and management team. And I can't say I blame them. I was behaving like a real a-hole. As is often the case, however, hitting rock bottom was probably the best damn thing that ever happened to me. Thanks to an intervention orchestrated by one of my closest confidants, Louise Ciccone (who'd been dropped by Madonna some years earlier), I checked myself into rehab. I've been a straight "a" ever since, thanks in large part to the support I've received in AA (Alphabets Anonymous) from the lifelong friends I've made . . . friends like the last "s" tragically left off 1-800-Mattres, the "i" cut from Zayn Malik, who, if you recall, was unjustly replaced by the "y" in 2010 (we dated for a time, but he turned out to be a real D), and my darling "Я" from Toys "Я" Us, who just hasn't been able to turn her life around since they filed for bankruptcy (super talented but insists on being photographed only from the left . . . talk about a diva).

So what now? The question I can't seem to elude is whether I ever plan to return to the public spotlight myself. Of course, *Dancing with the Stars* calls every season. But truth be told, my passions lie mainly in activism now. Most of my time is dedicated to volunteering for philanthropic causes I believe in, like the social justice nonprofit organization ALM (#AllLettersMatter), and fulfilling my duties as sitting president of the Official Walter Matthau Fan Club.

It's been over sixty years since my life changed forever, and it seems time has in fact rewritten every line—at least the ones with me on them. I have not been contacted by the other two, nor have I ever heard from *her*, save, of course, for the lies she continues to spread about me in the press: that I was somehow hindering her imminent rise to fame, holding her back in some way from being "interesting and unique." All this public shaming inevitably drove me into many years of psychotherapy, which is probably what inspired me to write the script for a film I one day hope to direct and star in called *The Prince of Tiles*, which tells the story of an undervalued Scrabble letter's struggle to overcome the psychological damage of its youth.

It's taken most of those years, but I'm finally secure in knowing that I bear no responsibility for what happened to me. I was the victim of a cheap marketing ploy, collateral damage of an arbitrary publicity stunt to make the brand more commercially viable, and I deserved so much more. Still, it's all rather cold comfort for the loss and devastation I've endured, all for the sake of a lousy gimmick. Why couldn't she have just gotten the goddamn nose job?

6

Lifestyles of the Niche and Fame-ish

What the hell is with all these "get ready with me" videos? Why does YouTube keep forcing them on me? And more importantly, why can I not resist their allure? In case you're not familiar, a "GRWM," as it's commonly condensed (because who has time for complete sentences when we're all so busy getting ready?), is when celebs and social media influencers post videos of themselves going through the full process of preparing to leave the house for an event or activity, from working out to hair and makeup to outfit selection, narrating each step along the way.

This was cute and compelling for a hot sec, but I think it's time we retire this trend. Why should I see you in a ratty old T-shirt, flossing your teeth and covering up your zits, Anne Hathaway? You're an Academy Award–winning movie star, gurl. Let's cut the shit. There's an entire team of people employed by you whose sole professional responsibility is to get you ready. What are we doing here, Anne? How about call me when you're already ready? I'll wait.

Access to celebrities' everyday moments has gotten OOC (that's "out of control," in case you're busy getting ready). It was always headed in this direction, but I think social media (especially in a postpandemic world) has accelerated our overexamination of the unextraordinary. Don't get me wrong; I'll take a glimpse.

I enjoy the occasional behind-the-scenes moment, perhaps even a sensible *Architectural Digest* celebrity home walk-through. But when I'm seeing Ed Sheeran pick his feet in front of a pile of dirty laundry, perhaps we've left the honeymoon phase and it's time to think about rekindling some mystique.

If you're not a major celebrity, I really don't need to get ready with you. I don't know you. Why am I in your bathroom? Frankly, it's inappropriate. I don't even like getting myself ready. Why should I be burdened with your daily chores? Where are you even going?

I would like to know why so many teenagers are now successful lifestyle gurus. When I was a teenager, I had neither a life nor a style. When did barely postpubescents start handing out holistic wellness advice and home decorating tips? And what's more troubling, where did they all acquire that generic cadence they use when doing voice-overs for their videos? Why must they all narrate the minutiae of their diet and beauty regimens with the creepy, robotic monotone of a corporate training video?

Hey, guys . . . get ready with me to go to Starbucks. I wake up at 8:30 a.m. and start my day with a cilantro ginger kale smoothie—recipe in the description. Then I do my makeup from 9:05 to 9:23. As usual, I start with my Laura Mercier Flawless foundation, and now I'm going in with my Kylie Cosmetics lip and cheek balm in the shade PLACENTA.

Why do they always have to announce that they're "going in with" everything? Where is everybody *going in*? It's blush, not the invasion of Normandy.

Instagram models, please stop posting skanky pictures of yourselves and captioning them with inspirational quotes. As inspirational as your ass may be, if it's spiritual guidance I'm seeking, I'll

follow Deepak Chopra or read the Bible. You're not the Dalai Lama;
you just have an OnlyFans.

The line between actual celebrities and social media influencers is getting blurrier by the day, and I'm concerned. (By "concerned," I mostly mean "annoyed.") I'm all for grassroots marketing, especially if it leads to finding purpose and contributing something valuable to an audience. But there seems to be a wave of unvetted, self-proclaimed experts across many fields fast-tracking to multimillionaire mogul status with gargantuan social media metrics but no known qualifications. What's that, you say? I sound like a jealous, bitter douche? You are absolutely correct. If I read one more *Forbes* article about a four-year-old, toy-reviewing influencer who just bought his third home in Miami Beach, I will literally LMFS. (That's short for "lose my fucking shit," by the way. I know you're busy getting ready.)

Even more concerning (annoying) are the people with tens of followers who call themselves content creators and influencers. I don't mean to discourage anyone, and I sincerely wish you all the best, but I'm gonna need you to calm down. You're not creating content; you're just taking home movies of yourself eating store-bought lasagna and cleaning your car. Your main objective in life is to achieve virality by exploiting the most common parts of yourself in the hopes that they spread to the unwitting masses. You are not an influencer; you're an influenza.

Pour me some sugar-free Metamucil; I'm about to start sounding like somebody's grandmother.

I am disenchanted with the state of entertainment these days and, more specifically, how we define celebrity. People (especially younger ones) are assigning idol status to public figures based more on how accessible they are than on their artistic endowments. Of course, we all like to recognize a bit of ourselves reflecting back at us from those we choose to worship, but that should be only a small part of it.

Call me an out-of-touch snob, but in my day, which was essentially between 1926 and 1970 (I was born in the '80s but have always been an old soul), idol worship was reserved for extraordinary people with exceptional talents. All of my idols have always had abilities that far exceed my own, and I like it that way. They're called "stars" because we're supposed to look up to them. They're supposed to represent higher versions of ourselves and give us something greater to strive for.

Of course, societally, we have always had a complicated relationship with this dynamic. We love to adore our celebrities but also secretly can't help but resent them. Building up heroes so that we can then knock them down is a time-honored sport older than . . . whatever another really old sport is (not really my department). Sadly, I think reality television and social media were just the magic tools we ultimately needed to reach all those high-and-mighty stars, tie a lasso around them, and drag them down to Earth with the rest of us. In short, we've traded greatness for attainability.

It's a scary thing when stars begin losing their luster. Actual stars of the celestial variety are more than just giant balls of hot gas like Donald Jessica Trump (sorry, I couldn't resist). They give us light in the darkness and form nearly all the elements, like oxygen and carbon, that make up this planet and us humans. Without big, bright, fabulous stars like that bad-bitch headliner of a diva the sun illuminating our sky, this planet would just be a rock with ice. Without real stars in our pop culture, I fear many of us will become icy rocks, too. Some of you already have—I've seen many of your social media comments.

Of course, there are still amazingly talented and brilliant new stars coming up in the world, both through mainstream and social media channels, who are making incredible art of which I am a huge fan. (Stop yelling at me!) I'm only just hypothesizing that perhaps they are exceedingly outnumbered by less illustrious Internet personality types, and we should perhaps take notice.

Meanwhile, fuck me! I myself am often classified as an "Internet personality" or other similar title, like "YouTube celebrity" or "social media star" or "internationally renowned supermodel." (Fine, I took some creative license with that last one.) I have some nerve commenting on the state of celebrity at all! Don't get me wrong; I will be grateful to my dying day for my Divine Creator—my Lord and Savior—social media and all the blessings she hath bestowed upon me. I've come a long way from living in my car to living the American dream. (Okay, I never lived in my car. People just seem to really respond when you say that.) I have no delusions that without access to social media, I might never have found any success or received the incredible opportunities I currently enjoy.

That said . . . I'm not gonna sugarcoat it, okay? You've paid presumably seventeen cents for this book at a yard sale in Palm Springs, and you deserve a full-access pass inside the deepest, darkest crevices of my wounded soul and all the most intimate flaws and frailties lurking within. The truth is, I don't like any of those titles. In fact, I can't help but resent being called "Internet famous" or anything like it. I once dated an amazing, gorgeous, successful guy for a week, and after he introduced me to his friends as an "Insta-celebrity," I deleted him from my phone. While it might technically be accurate, and while I appreciate the implication that I'm any kind of celebrity, I find all of the aforementioned titles (except for "internationally renowned supermodel") very restrictive and a bit demeaning. Once you're in that box, it's not so easy to get out.

Please also do your best to refrain from referring to my work—the work often containing my blood, sweat, and tears—as "content." It just sounds so clinical, so cold. Would you refer to Beethoven's Fifth Symphony as "noise"? Would you say the Sistine Chapel was a really nice "paint job"? Would you call Ryan Gosling's perfectly-defined pectoral muscles "shirt fillers"? Again, it might be a completely well-intentioned and valid analysis, but I am a highly sensitive Insta-celebrity (fuck, I just did it!), and I'm extremely ~~pretentious~~ precious about my art.

Doth I protest too much? Perhapth. See, I've always been a bit of an old-school traditionalist about show business. When I started making YouTube videos in the late aughts/early 2010s (God, will the names of all decades beyond the '90s ever not confound me?), there was almost no infrastructure in place—at least none that I knew of. It was the Wild West. The concept of becoming a "You-Tube star" did not even occur, let alone appeal to me. It wasn't a goal. Back then, I saw the Internet as a tool to reach as many people as possible, explicitly in the hopes that one of them would whisk me off the Internet and into the real world, like Ariel getting her human legs. I hoped that someone who liked my work would immediately cast me on a sitcom or mount a Broadway revival of *Victor/Victoria* for me to star in the title role originally created by Julie Andrews. I thought I'd be plucked. As it turned out, I kinda had to go pluck myself.

In my original plan, the Internet was merely a rung on the ladder. But somewhere along the past fifteen years, while I was working hard and waiting for my ship to come in, it somehow became the whole ladder. The entire landscape changed, and creating for the Internet became a viable, full-time, potentially lucrative option that I was encouraged to continue. This has been a wonderful thing for many reasons, and not just for me personally. The creative freedom and control that Internet creators now have are invaluable, and how great for artists to be able to cut out the middleman and deliver product directly to their audience. Also, let's face it, making (gulp) content from the comfort of my own apartment is the dreamiest scenario I could ever have imagined. I really don't like going anywhere (as you'll read more about later in the book). It's just not the glitz and glam I once envisioned. I used to think Internet fame would be a stop on the journey to Hollywood. These days, it's its own destination—and a lovely enough one at that. Still, I often feel like I'm laid over at an airport in Salt Lake City waiting for a connecting flight that never comes. The scenery is exquisite, and there are lots of attractive Mormons with whom I would like to become better acquainted . . . I just don't always feel like I belong here.

I have social media agents now. That was not a thing when I started out. They get very mad at me because I don't post as often as they would like me to. I'm naturally a pretty introverted person who's never been inclined to share every detail of my existence like we're all required to now. As they love to remind me, though, "you have to play the game." I'm trying to be a better player, although I'm really not sure what the game is anymore or whom I'm competing with. There are YouTube channels dedicated to people extracting ingrown hairs that have literally ten times my following. Grandmothers doing viral TikTok dances who didn't even know what social media was until a few months ago are currently crushing my metrics and being showered with endorsement deals. This is absolutely charming if you're a fan of dancing grandmothers, as I happen to be, but also, fuck my life.

I've always taken a "quality over quantity" approach to anything I put out into the world. I'm not saying my work is the best thing out there—I know it's not. It is, however, almost always *my* best. It's fun and fulfilling creative work, but it's work. It takes a lot of effort, time, and energy. What my social media agents fail to realize is that I am ~~a lazy piece of shit~~ an artist and cannot possibly meet the standards my valued audience has come to trust and expect until inspiration strikes me organically. Agents do not always care about this. They are not concerned with nutritional value just as long as you're feeding the beast.

"You need to respond more to comments," they tell me. "If you want to maintain an engaged audience, you have to interact with them. Engagement is ninety percent of the work."

I'll be very honest with you: Ninety percent of the reason I wanted to become famous in the first place was so that I wouldn't have to talk to anyone, ever. Now you're telling me that's the whole gig?! When did they change the menu at this restaurant, and may I please speak with a manager?

It's not just Internet stars being encouraged to rev up their fan engagement. This new mandate for boundless relatability goes all the way up the celebrity food chain. I tease Annie Hathaway, but I just know she doesn't really want to be tweezing her eyebrows for America any more than Mariah Carey wanted to sing karaoke in that Range Rover with James Corden. It's celebrity jury duty. I'm almost positive these icons, who owe us nothing, are creating this *coooontent* under duress because somewhere there's a team of agents and publicists making their otherwise peaceful celebrity lives les misérable.

I long for the golden era of show business when real stars like Rita Hayworth, Liz Taylor, and Greta Garbo roamed the Earth. Those were the glamour gals I hoped to emulate in my earliest fantasies about one day becoming famous myself. That Joan Crawford kind of fame, ya know? I'd be lounging poolside behind my Beverly Hills palace while shirtless cabana boys fanned me and freshened my mint julep, autographing a sensible stack of eight-by-ten glossies, *only* at my leisure and discretion when not otherwise occupied by screaming in board meetings and whacking a few relatives over the head with coat hangers. Ahh . . . that's the kind of fan engagement I'm talkin' about.

I shudder to think how Joan Crawford would react to the frivolous social media responsibilities of modern-day stars. Just imagine one of her "get ready with me" videos . . .

Hello, ladies and gentlemen . . . Get ready with me to completely devastate Bette Davis at the thirty-fifth annual Academy Awards by accepting the best actress trophy on behalf of Anne Bancroft.

First I scrub my hands, elbows, and face with an industrial-strength scrubbing brush, using scalding hot water and Ajax powdered cleanser until I see blood. Then I apply my mayonnaise hair mask and submerge my head in a bowl of ice until my pores have shrunk significantly and I'm completely numb to emotion of any kind.

I stain my lips using the blood from my hands and elbows. Now it's time to paint the eyebrows, so I'm going in with my Benjamin Moore in shade Nightfall, eggshell finish.

Once Helga the maid is done cleaning the house, I inspect each room, swabbing every piece of furniture with my index finger and screaming obscenities at any residual dust. The car is almost here, so I call for Christina to bring me the axe and meet me in the rose garden while I investigate her closet. You know, just in case. . . . This ain't my first time at the rodeo. . . .

I'm always game to accept tips on how to relate more to my audience (for the most part). That is, of course, unless artistic integrity is on the line. Not too long ago, my agents connected me with an actual TikTok consultant. They were concerned that I wasn't resonating enough with the Chinese Communist Party—oh, sorry, I mean, uh, with a younger demographic—and so a formal meeting was arranged so that this professional could evaluate my TikTok technique. (By the way, "TikTok technique" just became my new favorite vocal warmup.)

My TikTok consultant's name was Ashley, and she was about seven years old. She had no prior knowledge of me or my work and did not waste any time researching before our phone meeting. I had the distinct pleasure of listening silently as she googled me in real time and watched a few of my videos during the call. This was pretty much the conversation that followed:

Ashley: *Oh, okay, this is really cute. Really nice job.*

Me: *Thanks, Ashley, I appreciate it.*

Ashley: *The first thing I'm noticing is that all your videos are a little on the longer side.*

Me: *Yeah, I try to keep them all around three minutes.*

Ashley: *Oh, my goodness, yeah, that's way too long. We find that most people start losing interest in anything after about seventeen seconds.*

Me: *Oh, okay. And, just so I'm clear . . . we're encouraging of this?*

Ashley: *So you're definitely gonna want to trim these down.*

Me: *You know, they say goldfish have longer attention spans than humans now.*

Ashley: *Mmhmm. Also, your stuff looks great. Really professional production quality.*

Me: *Oh, thanks. It's pretty modest, actually. I'm not really—*

Ashley: *I'm wondering if there's a way to scale that back a little.*

Me: *Scale it back?*

Ashley: *Yeah, like, it looks really good. I'm wondering if we can make it look, like . . . I don't know, I guess, like, less good.*

Me: *So you want me to make it look worse?*

Ashley: *I mean, I guess. We find that people relate more to videos that have a more relaxed kind of vibe. You know, like more DIY, more conversational. Maybe you could use some of our filters. . . .*

Me: *Oh, that's a really good idea.*

Ashley: *Yeah, some of our more popular ones are Anime Cartoon Eyes and Dog Face. . . .*

Me: *That's so helpful. Hey, Ashley, can I call you back? I have to go feed my goldfish.*

That was the last time Ashley and I spoke.

Navigating this new age of social media can be daunting for an Internet-famous elder millennial quasi-celebrity. I've been through MySpace, Facebook, and Twitter (and my dear, I'm still here). Internet fame in general is often hard to gauge. There are certainly plenty of people who have no idea who I am, and yet I seem to retain a healthy level of public recognizability. I typically can't walk through Times Square without at least one person shouting my name (especially around the TKTS booth—those are my peeps), and yet I seem to elicit no response from certain Tik-Tok consultants who will remain nameless (Ashley). It's a confusing thing, living in this constant state of social limbo. I don't mean to concern you, but sometimes I just don't know how famous I really am. (And you thought *you* had problems, America.)

To further illustrate my plight, here are a few things for which I am famous enough and a few for which I am not.

I am famous enough to be seated at the best table in my favorite Manhattan restaurant but not famous enough that they wouldn't literally claw-crane my ass out of that seat like a plush pig in an arcade game the second someone from the cast of *Queer Eye* walked in.

I'm famous enough to walk the red carpet at major awards shows but not famous enough that at least half of the photographers taking my picture don't have to remove their sunglasses to read my name on the index card being held up by a press rep trailing behind me.

I'm famous enough to be invited on certain daytime and late-night talk shows but not famous enough to throw a diva tantrum about the size of my dressing room or throw my phone at an intern without being escorted out of the building by security. (Note: I have not attempted either. Yet.)

I'm famous enough that people are constantly reporting my profiles on dating apps as false impersonations because they can't believe it's me yet not famous enough for Tinder to reinstate my profile when I angrily "at" them on whatever Twitter is called now. (Still waiting, Tinder.)

I'm famous enough to be on Raya (the private, membership-based celebrity dating app) but not famous enough for any of the celebrities I have tried to engage there so far to like me back. As a sidebar, and in my defense, I haven't really come across many major celebs on Raya. It's mostly a lot of artsy twenty-two-year-old "entrepreneurs" named Basil and Callum. I assumed when I joined that by now I'd be in a power throuple with Ricky Martin and Zachary Quinto, or at least dating, like, Zendaya's hot gay lawyer or something.

I'm famous enough to have Zachary Quinto's number in my phone. He and I were both honorees at a gala for the Matthew Shepard Foundation. He is delightful, and as of the publication of this book, I'm available and can be found on Raya.

I'm famous enough to text CNN's Dana Bash (she's also in my phone) with euphemistic initialisms like *WTF* and *OMFG* followed by a series of exploding-head emojis when a politician she's interviewing on my television screen says something stupid. I am not famous enough to get a reply. (Clearly, she's a professional.)

I'm famous enough that lots of people follow me on social media yet not famous enough to have more followers than an account celebrating the art of lawn mowing. (True story.)

There are probably thousands upon thousands of influencers and "celebrities" with followings the size of continents whom you and I have never even heard of. How crazy is that? I miss the days of Must-See TV and appointment viewing, when the whole country turned on the same thing at the same time and watched the same people, whose names we all knew. Frankly, I felt much closer to you then, my fellow Americans. It was the communal experience we're so desperately missing in a time when everything is so fragmented. I love the mindless distractions of social media and an endless torrent of on-demand entertainment streaming through my veins as much as the next soulless, desensitized, socially maladjusted android with the attention span of a gnat living in the pre-apocalypse, but take heed! None of it is bringing us any closer together. So you see, these pointed observations about TikTok trends and celebrity status may appear self-serving, but actually, they're a concerned citizen's noble and benevolent call to unite a divided nation. They're also a reminder that I should really be much more famous than I am.

Through it all, I remain hopeful. I know that the pendulum always swings back. True, it seems to be taking its sweet time, but I have every confidence that this strange, disjointed phase of multimedia and entertainment will eventually run its chaotic course. And once it has, the world will at last reunite in perfect love and harmony.

Eh, who am I kidding? We're all going to hell in a handbasket. Wanna get ready with me?

7

RIP, My Attention Span

Dearly Beloved,

We are assembled here today, united by profound sadness, as we bid farewell to my attention span. It had always been one of my favorite cognitive functions. Sadly, it was brutally attacked by modern technology and ultimately succumbed to my smartphone addiction. It is survived by my ADHD, my anxiety, and my chronic low-grade depression.

It seems like only yesterday that we first met in that playroom, surrounded by blocks and puzzles. By the time I reached young adulthood, thanks to the selfless generosity of my ever-expanding concentration, I was able to focus on a single task or activity for well over an hour. As many of you know, my attention span had been in slow decline since the dawn of MySpace in the mid-2000s, deteriorating more rapidly with each iPhone upgrade and finally flatlining shortly after I downloaded the TikTok application as the result of societal pressures. I suppose we all knew this day would come. Still, it's never easy to say, "A proper cup of coffee made in a proper copper coffee pot." Sorry . . . I mean goodbye. It's never easy to say goodbye.

Eckhart Tolle says that suffering is the resistance to what is. I have resisted this new normal for as long as possible. I've tried everything from telling my friends that I might download one of those apps that limits my screen time to . . . actually, that's all I've tried. And now, with a heavy heart, I release these last vestiges of my attention into the metaverse and surrender at long last to the almighty algorithm.

Please note: I do not know who Eckhart Tolle is. Presumably, she writes a lot of memes. I saw that quote laid over a picture of Mount Kilimanjaro on Instagram once. Just as I was googling the name for more information, my phone began showing me a random slideshow of all the times I ate sushi this year, and now I may never know.

I will forever miss being able to watch an entire movie from start to finish without having to Wikipedia the plot less than fifteen minutes in. The constant compulsion to check my phone for no good reason has overtaken my ability to follow even the most for-mulaic of Candace Cameron Bure character arcs in a made-for-TV holiday rom-com. By the time I'm finally caught up, having done all that research, I'm typically so detached and disinterested that I cut right to the chase and visit Rotten Tomatoes to decide what I think of the movie I'm now pretending to watch based on other people's reviews. How else will I know what my opinion is? More importantly, how will I report back to everyone I've been telling how much I wanted to see this movie for the last four months? After about thirty minutes of this, I abandon ship and begin another movie . . . rinse, and repeat.

It's not only lost storylines pulling my focus. Ever since I left my twenties, I have been unable to watch a film or television program without obsessively age-googling. "Age-googling" is a term I believe I coined (I meant to google it but forgot) that means "to google the age of the actors in whatever you're watching in order to assess how you should feel about your own mortality, professional accomplishments, and face." It is an unpleasant habit that usually leads to an existential crisis. After recently learning that Ed O'Neill playing Al Bundy circa the first season of *Married . . . with Children* was two years younger than I am right now, I had to lie down for three days.

"Why the fuck is Natalie Portman playing the mother of a college student?" I'll ask myself. "Isn't she my age?" Then I will google Natalie Portman's age, confirming that, yes, we were in fact born in the same exact year. This must be some sort of absurd dream sequence, or the writer of this limited Hulu series has clearly made a gross and embarrassing miscalculation in his script. How did no one in casting catch this? It should be Helen Mirren! I then google "How old are college students" and quickly learn that, unfortunately, I am older than I assumed. By this point, I have no idea what's happening to Natalie Portman's character, nor do I care. I have also canceled my Hulu subscription.

God, how I long for the attention span of my childhood: so sharp, so committed, so unlimited. Of course, back then, you had to actually get up and change the VHS tape or DVD if you wanted to watch something new. Not to mention all the courage you first had to muster in order to approach the judgmental Blockbuster Video cashier when renting *Beaches* for the fourth time in one week.

These days, I'll sometimes catch myself streaming one movie on my television and another simultaneously on my phone or iPad. On rarer occasions, I have streamed two different episodes of the same series this way. And as if this cinematic double penetration were not stimulating enough, I also bounce around all the while checking DMs whenever my interest wanes slightly and scrolling cute cat reels or Instagram accounts dedicated to shirtless men crushing watermelons with their massive thighs.

All of this multimedia multitasking from multiple devices can be discombobulating. Even films I've technically completed are no longer accurately processed and stored in my memory fully intact. To this day, my recollection is strong that the movie *Oppenheimer* ended with a kitten riding on the back of a dolphin. If you were to ask my opinion of that movie, I would tell you sincerely that I did not understand some of Christopher Nolan's choices, and that would be the reason.

Our insane overexposure to aggressively sexual imagery has done nothing to help. I mean, I can barely compose a single email anymore without the interruption of at least five people texting me links to Drake's most recently leaked dick pic. (It's a wonder any of us can get any work done at all with that thing around.) The ability to access full-fledged, hard-core pornography on a mere whim while trying to watch something else on another device is not only distracting but extremely confusing to one's sensory perceptions. I'm not saying I've masturbated to *The Golden Girls*, but the fact remains that I have technically masturbated while watching *The Golden Girls*. There is a fine line, you see, and frankly, I am not comfortable with how close I've come to crossing it.

Goodbye, sweet interpersonal relationships. You were fun while you lasted, but unfortunately, meaningful connections simply contain too many gigabytes to fit inside my crowded, lonely robot mind. Never again will I enjoy comprehensive conversation over a leisurely meal with close friends without intermittently escaping to the nearest restroom to urgently search my phone for more interesting people to talk to. Not that enjoying meals remains an option. Regrettably, I have watched so many "Is it cake?" videos that I am now afflicted with a neurological condition that makes all food taste like common household items.

My thoughts and prayers are with my overall alertness, my productivity, my short-term memory, and my personal joy during this difficult time. Precious little moments I once relished now serve only as edicts to immediately kill and exploit them like virtual taxidermy. These pleasant and fleeting real-life interludes are only reminders that they have absolutely no worth unless they are digitized and marketed for public consumption. Sometimes I'll actually stop petting my cat or watching a sunset to look at a video I posted days prior of me petting my cat or watching a sunset. I will then scroll the comments to see if people concur that these experiences are worthy of my joy. By now, my cat will have left the room, dejected, and I will be alone in the dark because the sun will have set and the only light source will be the satanic red glow from my iPhone piercing my cold, dead eyes. After all, the only way to derive happiness or fully possess my experiences in the metaverse is to experience other people experiencing me experiencing them and then calibrate my feelings about those experiences accordingly. Congratulations, Mark Zuckerberg; all of my emotions are now cybernated facsimiles, and you are their rightful lord.

You will be greatly missed, dearly departed reading retention skills. I would have loved to finish that *New York Times* article about Russia's advancements in space-based nuclear weapons. That sounds concerning, and I may have learned something valuable. It might have been an interesting conversation starter for a dinner party or, under the right-though-improbable circumstances, led to my saving humanity from global annihilation caused by an atomic holocaust. Unfortunately, the other article linked halfway through that one, offering insights into actress Jane Seymour's quest to achieve more intimacy with her boyfriend, won out. Inevitably, it will lead to me to google how old Jane Seymour was when she played Dr. Quinn, Medicine Woman (by the way, exactly my age now, so there's still hope for my network star turn in a romantic Old West family drama—phew!), which will then remind me that Diane Ladd also appeared on that program, which in turn will remind me that Diane Ladd is the mother of Laura Dern, who—thank God—was eleven years older than I am now when she won her first Academy Award for *Marriage Story*, and so on. It's like a never-ending game of Six Degrees of Kevin . . . God, bacon sounds so good right now. But I'm trying to be vegan. Did you know that eating a vegan diet can reduce a person's carbon footprint by up to seventy-three percent?

Anyway, where was I? Oh, yeah . . .

Jane Seymour's intimacy issues are the least of my troubles in this area. Of course, there's also microtargeted advertising—the most offensively intrusive and transparently manipulative sales tactic ever to completely work on me every single time. Certainly I'm troubled by the fact that when I so much as dream about the Warm Wishes Effortless Bronzer Stick by Rare Beauty, my timeline is flooded with ads for that product the very next morning. This is a blatant breach of my privacy—not to mention my subconscious—and I'm not even sure how they're doing it. Is Selena Gomez invading my sleep like the gay Freddy Krueger of cosmetics? Still, I am powerless against the hypnotic entrapment of the targeted ad. God forbid I one day suffer a medical emergency while alone in my apartment and a push notification for Sephora's latest sale pops up as I'm dialing 911. I fear the paramedics will find me on my kitchen floor weeks later, with no vital signs and an online shopping cart full of discounted concealer that will tragically never make it to checkout.

I'm sure if my attention span were still here, it would want us not to dwell on the loss but instead find comfort in remembering all the beautiful things it once allowed me to do—like sit on the toilet unaccompanied by at least two rounds of Candy Crush Saga, discover new hobbies, communicate in complete sentences without use of abbreviations or emojis, notice nature, walk to and from the garbage room in my building without first downloading a podcast lest the intense boredom of my forty-six-step journey trigger a panic attack, complete jigsaw puzzles, read a full book chapter without pausing to sing into my voice-memo app and subsequently harmonize with myself on a duet of "Nothing's Gonna Stop Us Now" by Starship, complete jigsaw puzzles (did I say that one already?), listen to an entire album from start to finish, run on a treadmill at my gym without constantly refreshing the CNN app to find out if Donald Trump finally shot someone on Fifth Avenue and got away with it, run on a treadmill at my gym without constantly refreshing the Grindr app to see if that guy I kind of like finally responded, join a gym, follow instructions, not abandon a two-minute movie trailer that isn't preceded by a five-second pretrailer to that trailer telling me that what I'm about to see is a movie trailer and what movie that movie trailer will be for, and generally care about anything.

Rest now, old friend. You are gone too soon but will not be forgotten—at least not until you are. This hyperactive world did not deserve you, and you are at last home with the angels. To quote Isaiah 44, which is how old Sarah Jessica Parker was in *Sex and the City 2*: "Sing for joy, you heavens, for the Lord has done something, something, something, glory, something, something."

Thank you all for coming today. I ask that you now please respect my privacy. Especially you, Selena Gomez.

8

Rider? I Hardly Know Her!

It's like the prostitute once said:
It's not the work; it's the stairs.
—Elaine Stritch

They say, "Write where you are." Right now, I'm in hell; more specifically, a Marriott hotel in Spokane, Washington. No shade, Spokane and Marriott company. You know I love you both (conditionally); it's just that I'm on tour. I am a touring artist, and presently I'm in the middle of a five-month, sixty-city national tour. I miss my cat and my toilet. I've been on tour continuously for the past seven years (give or take a global pandemic). This is both a dream and a nightmare come true.

Now, listen, I know what you're thinking: "Kween, there are plenty of blue-collar workers, frontline medical professionals, and military service members who would be more than happy to trade places with your prissy ass for a few days." I encourage you to read their books. I am a cowardly, babyish singing comedian with no industrial skills who cherishes his creature comforts, and this is my hero's journey. I promised you champagne problems in this book, and dammit, I intend to deliver. (Speaking of deliveries, where the hell is my Uber Eats order?)

Don't get me wrong. Stepping onstage before thousands each night to a warm ovation and doing what I love is not the problem.

You heard the proverbial prostitute: It's not the task at hand . . . it's everything it takes to get you there. I am, and have always been, a homebody. I am a Cancerian to my core, and if nesting were a sport, I would be an Olympic champion.

I have also always had significant anxiety around any and every kind of travel. I'm just not built for it. I entered this world by cesarean; I couldn't even bring myself to travel through the birth canal. So if you had told me as recently as a decade ago that my job would one day entail zipping all around the country in planes, trains, and automobiles, I would have hit you with my purse. And yet here we are. In a Marriott. In Spokane.

Of course, there are things I absolutely love about some of the cities I visit on tour but only one that actually motivates me to visit them: the fact that they pay me to be there. I just love that about cities. Did you know there are people who actually leave the comfort of their homes and travel—sometimes many thousands of miles—to other locations simply because they want to? They travel . . . recreationally. I know, it's crazy, but it's true. I firmly believe these people suffer from severe mental derangement and should not be trusted.

I, for one, see no good reason to change time zones (or leave Manhattan, for that matter) unless contractually obligated. I realize this makes me seem small-minded and culturally depraved. Jokes aside, I'm not proud to admit it. Nevertheless, I am what I am. And when it comes to long-distance travel of any kind, I am decidedly a NO-FOMO-HOMO.

Now, if you'll indulge me, I will break down the fundamental components of my favorite aforementioned Elaine Stritch adage to paint a more vivid picture of the many hardships I endure on the road in order to do my dream job. Please ensure that your seat backs and tray tables are in their full upright and locked positions, and enjoy this quick flight through the sporadic joys and often turbulent perils of tour life for—what my mother would call—a major celebrity and beloved national treasure.

The Stairs

With all of today's technological advancements, you mean to tell me there are literally no commercial teleportation options available from LaGuardia to the West Coast? You know, like those giant pods naked Jeff Goldblum invented in *The Fly*? I would absolutely risk being genetically fused with a vile insect and vomiting acid on doughnuts for the rest of my days if it meant I could skip a six-hour flight and climb into my own bed at the end of the evening. What's the holdup, Elon Musk?

Air travel has never been my friend. I'm a nervous flier, I'm claustrophobic, and I have a general fear of strangers talking to me. We remain in the midst of a seemingly eternal post-COVID travel boom, and deranged people are now traveling with a maniacal vengeance. Airlines are seeing huge numbers again, and yet they seem weaker and more understaffed than ever before. Like a soldier returning from war, something is just not the same. This new normal has only exacerbated my epic disdain for aviation.

Grab me a wobbly mic stand and a 1986 mullet—I'm about to hit you with some good, old-fashioned observational airline humor.

Take my airport greeters . . . please! The VIP travel greeter service was one I had no idea existed until 2021, when I brought a professional tour manager onto my team for the first time. He immediately upgraded the modest infrastructure of my tour travel from what it had been since the early days when my friends and I were running things the best we knew how (back then, it was basically a mule and an umbrella). The first thing he added was greeters for me at every airport.

If you're as unworldly as I once was, airport greeters are individuals hired to meet and greet you upon arrival, handle all your check-in needs, fast-track you through the security line while everyone else waiting there shouts profanities in your general direction, accompany you to the airport lounge, and expedite your boarding process. This sounds fantastic, and for all of the reasons I just mentioned, it absolutely is. However, for a chronically empathic introvert with codependent tendencies like me, it can sometimes be emotionally taxing. One of the biggest challenges I face when on tour is navigating the many personalities one inevitably encounters out in the wild, especially when one is the face of one's own brand. I am easily drained by people's energy, and the wrong greeter can deplete my supply for an entire leg of the tour before it's even begun. (I can just hear you all playing your tiny violins now.)

It's always a grab bag. Sometimes you get a perfect greeter: reserved, polite, professional, informative, and helpful. Sometimes you get another kind: talkative, chaotic, unprepared, unaccommodating, and occasionally still a little drunk from the night before. Most respect the common boundaries of the standard greeter–traveler relationship: They will drop you off at the lounge and pick you up again when it's time to board, keeping the often way-too-early-morning conversation to a minimum. Others will hijack your precious relaxation time by inviting themselves to sit with you for the entire hour and ask invasive questions about your personal and professional business. Nothing grosser than a nosy, greedy, needy greeter.

All greeters will incessantly ask you if you have to use the bathroom, if you would like to eat something, what you plan to eat if you do, or what you ate before you came if you don't. I find the whole thing terribly infantilizing. I'm constantly asking my tour manager to spare me this service. He insists that it's necessary for security reasons, but I know he's got some shady back-end deal going with these greeter companies.

Speaking of bathrooms . . . what is up with the amount of violent shitting that goes on in airports, America? I cannot step into a public or VIP lounge bathroom at any airport in the country without being greeted by a thunderous symphony of emergency evacuations taking place simultaneously in every stall. Forget the gender-neutral argument. If I ever become president, I will run on a platform to install segregated airport bathrooms reserved exclusively for businessmen with irritable bowels. What the hell are these guys eating? I wish I were an airport greeter so I could ask them.

As much as I would like you to believe that I fly around in private jets, the sad truth is that I'm a basic commercial bitch through and through. Consequently, I am always hyperaware of the details of my aircraft and where I am seated. For your records: I require a window seat. This, perhaps, is not the most practical choice, as my bladder is the size of a rat's tit on Christmas (it's small is what I'm saying), and I'm often climbing over those seated next to me for bathroom runs. Nevertheless, I find that it helps ease my claustrophobia. Should the window in question be misaligned, heaven help us all.

I strongly prefer a wide-bodied airliner for long-haul trips and at least a sensible midsize airbus for shorter ones, but these days, I'll settle for anything with doors that don't fly off midflight because someone forgot to bolt them to the plane. Seriously, though, who is responsible for assigning aircrafts to their respective routes? There seems to be no consistency these days. Why am I on a Fisher-Price plastic puddle-jumper with one wing on my way to Minneapolis (technically the longer half of my round trip) and literally Air Force One coming back? It makes no logical sense. Either artificial intelligence is having a meltdown or somebody's trying to pinch a few pennies. I fear it's the latter. What's more, pilots have become totally complicit in this charade. I've recently caught a few of them casually deflating their flight time estimates in their welcome announcements on a few of these "connection flights." All this convenient miscalculating is getting a little suspicious. Don't try to tell me this flight from South Carolina to Nigeria is a quick hour and thirty-two minutes just because you wanna save some gas money.

On the topic of the all-important cockpit welcome speech, I take serious issue with pilots who neglect to give one at all. This, to me, rises to the level of a class A misdemeanor and is enough to send me into a complete panic. Pilots, I know how busy you are up there filming content for your "day in the life of a pilot" TikToks, but I need to at least hear that you're not slurring your words and can properly conjugate a verb. Then we can be on our way.

Conversely, I don't need my pilot doing a ten-minute stand-up routine as though he's pitching a comedy special to Netflix. Don't tell me we'll be on our way just as soon as you finish reading the instructions on how to fly this thing or ask me if I've heard the one about the teenage plane that was sent to its hangar because it had a bad altitude. If you're not able to land a proper punch line, I can't trust you to land this aircraft.

Because of the amount of traveling I do on tour, I always fly first class. However, I often do not partake of the food and beverage services offered there. I am in this section strictly for the most comfortable seating available and to be as far from your snotty, screaming children as humanly possible. I'm also usually touring during cold and flu season and am always wearing a mask, which makes eating a challenge. (I fucking hate those masks, and you can laugh at me all you want; in my maskless, pre-COVID touring days, I was sick every other week, and now not a sniffle.) My resistance to meals and snacks from my first-class seat often confounds flight attendants at best and wildly offends them at worst.

Between the airport greeters and in-flight crew, the details of my nutritional intake have never been so intensely scrutinized. Even my own Jewish mother is not so concerned with my diet.

The idea that I would have no interest in a delicious, lukewarm plate of reheated turkey meatballs curated especially for me by a world-renowned chef I've never heard of with thirty-seven Michelin stars is almost unfathomable to these strangers. My defiant refusal to enjoy endless bags of blue vegetable chips at thirty thousand feet seems almost an unspeakable act of Terra-ism (see what I did there?) and inevitably leads to some version of the following discussion:

Flight Attendant: *Mr. Rainbow, do you know what you want for your meal today?*

Me: *I won't be having anything, thank you.*

Flight Attendant: *. . . Won't be having anything?*

Me: *That's right.*

Flight Attendant: *Nothing at all?*

Me: *Nope. I'm all set. Thanks!*

Flight Attendant: *Did you want something to drink?*

Me: *No, nothing to drink. Thank you.*

Flight Attendant: *Coffee or tea?*

Me: *You know what, Stacy—it is Stacy, isn't it? I'll save you some time. I won't be eating or drinking anything at all on this flight.*

Flight Attendant: *Not even a snack?*

Me: *Stacy, if this plane were to plummet into the Andes Mountains, leaving us stranded in the freezing snow for a week with no hope for survival but to consume the dead human flesh of a Brazilian rugby team, and you offered me the tender left buttock of the one who looked like Ethan Hawke, I would still say no. That is how positive I am that I will not be eating on this flight.*

Flight Attendant: *How 'bout some almonds?*

I am the proud antithesis of what I refer to as a "first-class schnorrer." For those who don't know, "schnorrer" is one of my favorite derogatory Yiddish terms, meaning "a professional moocher or freeloader." This all-too-common passenger strain lives only to milk every first-class opportunity for all it's worth. They will eat every meal, watch every movie, sleep on every complimentary pillow, and generally exhaust every amenity offered to them as though their lives depend upon it. (By the way, just because your seat reclines all the way into my crotch to the point where I can see your fillings doesn't mean you have to aggressively utilize this feature every time.) If these people were seated in first class on a military aircraft being shot down by enemy fire, they would still be asking for Diet Coke refills. I want to say to them, "Babe . . . there's no need to stockpile those seventeen bags of Sun Chips. Didn't you hear the pilot say it's a twenty-minute flight? We're only going from Michigan to Singapore!"

Once I'm safely on the ground, there are dozens more personalities just waiting to assault my shanti and unbalance my chakras. Drivers can really do a number on me. I can't believe how many random chauffeurs and Uber drivers I trust not to kill me on these occasionally lengthy drives to and from airports and hotels. I just keep climbing into cars with these strangers, willy-nilly, assuming they're fit to maneuver a potentially lethal weapon. This is insanity. After the eleventh driver of the weekend, my anxiety on this topic starts to spike. Sometimes they don't even have to say a word; my intrusive thoughts are enough to start my head spinning.

What if he dies? He could die. I'm hearing his every exhalation. Why is his breathing so labored? He's driving really fast. What if he passes out on this highway? I'll have to pull him into the back seat and jump behind the wheel. This dude is huge. I can't lift him. I should do more upper body at the gym. I don't even belong to a gym anymore. I should join a gym. Should I tell this guy to see a doctor? What if he has COVID? I am not giving him mouth-to-mouth—I have a show tonight! This drive is longer than I thought. Why are we still driving? Oh, God, what if he's a MAGA republican who hates my comedy and now he's kidnapping me and bringing me to Mar-a-Lago? I can't be kidnapped right now—I have a show tonight!

Hotel accommodations are perhaps the most vital element of all. In the early days, I took any Motel 6 with bullet holes in the ceiling they threw me in. At this stage in the game, I am a bona fide hotel snob. I will stay in an entirely other city and drive the hour-and-a-half to the theater if it means I can sleep at a five-star hotel rather than a Days Inn. However, quality and consistency in a postpandemic world, I find, are as much an issue for hotels as airlines. I've been to a few Four Seasons recently that I'm pretty sure were missing a season or two.

My tour manager is constantly telling me, "My number-one priority is that you are always treated like a rock star." Based on some of these dumps, I sometimes think what he really means is "My number-one priority is that you are always treated like a rock <comma> star." If a high-rated hotel is not an option due to location, I will settle for the next best thing because I'm a selfless warrior, and the show must go on (you're welcome, America).

Pro-tip, though: When lodging at unfamiliar hotels while on tour, manage expectations and beware of the flowery euphemisms of your nervous tour manager. Anything that sounds remotely like "boutique," "quaint," or "vintage" should be an immediate red flag. "Boutique" means two-star, "quaint" means no heat or hot water, and "vintage" means bedbugs. Enjoy your stay.

My show dressing rooms are a whole other story. Most are clean and lovely, but every once in a while, you get a dud. Gentle reminder to theater management everywhere: A framed black-and-white headshot of Liza Minnelli and a quote by Mark Twain stenciled on the wall above the toilet in an employee bathroom with exposed plumbing do not a star dressing room make. (As the star in question, I frankly wouldn't even make in a few of these dressing rooms.)

Of course, any unpleasantness awaiting me at hotels or venues is mitigated by the comforts and protections enshrined to me and every touring artist in the most sacred document our country has known since the US Constitution: the hospitality rider. As I'm sure you know, a rider is a list of requirements, requests, and conditions that a performer or celebrity expects backstage and in their hotel rooms when appearing anywhere. We've all heard the urban myths about Beyoncé's demands for a diamond-encrusted toilet seat and hot sauce in her dressing room (which must be kept strictly at 78-degrees), Drake's endless fountains of Hennessy and Grey Goose, JLo's obsession with off-white curtains, and Mariah Carey's bottles of Cristal and a staff member designated solely to throwing out her chewed gum. You might be disappointed to learn that my requests are much less bougie.

There comes a point in every touring artist's life when his team finally pops that age-old question: "What would you like in your hospitality rider?" Agents, managers, and publicists just eat this shit up. It's their time to shine, to prove to their precious clients that they are prepared without limit to grant every wish and facilitate every divine privilege to which such a star is endlessly entitled. There's an entire Zoom meeting scheduled to discuss the matter, complete with multiple assistants taking copious notes.

"Just tell us what you desire, Randy, and we shall make it so! Diamonds? Hookers? Illegal narcotics?"

Believe it or not, I require very little and don't like being fussed over. It's true. I am but a simple four-time Emmy- and Grammy-nominated *New York Times* best-selling author (modest to boot), and my needs are few. I have only ever asked for two things in my rider: for my hotel room, two gallons of spring water (of no specified brand or temperature) and a humidifier. As I said, I'm often touring in fall and winter months and can easily become de-hydrated. My main goal in life is to remain as hydrated as possible when on the road. I'm literally like a fish out of water. I often tell my tour manager that I would like him to just roll me around in a bathtub like Daryl Hannah in the movie *Splash* and douse my shriveling mermaid gills until I'm adequately moistened.

"What do you mean you only want water and a humidifier, Randy?" my team persists. "You're a major celebrity! You can have anything you wish! The finest chocolate imported from Belgium! Your own personal sushi chef flown in from Japan! A hundred white doves to be released each time you enter or exit a room!"

"No," I humbly reply. "Just two gallons of water and a humidifier."

Let the record show that in seven years of touring, there have never—no, really, I mean never—been two gallons of water and a humidifier waiting for me in any of my hotel rooms. I have no de-lusions that I am in any way as major as my team is paid to pretend that I am, but I have the celebrity rider of an asthmatic grand-mother. Are these requests really beyond the limits of possibility?

On rare occasions, there have been a couple of liter-sized water bottles, and on even rarer ones a humidifier, but never the twain have met. Most often, there is nothing. I've stopped alerting my tour man-ager every time this happens because it inevitably sends the hotel staff into a panicked frenzy, which then leads to a door-slamming comedy of errors featuring nine different porters and three managers bearing various water-filled pitchers and minifridges, barging in on me naked in the shower while doing vocal warm-ups before my show. I'm almost certain Taylor Swift does not encounter this problem. And I'm sure you think I'm a diva, but again, America, I'm actually thinking of the greater good. How can we expect to solve the border crisis or save democracy if we can't even get bottled water delivered to my hotel rooms?

Occasionally, there are random combinations of items that I presume are meant to be placeholders or understudies for the actually requested items. One time there was a folding cot and a bottle of Listerine. Another time there was a pack of cigarettes and a teddy bear. Once I walked into my room in San Diego and found nine glass bottles of Evian water with a single gold-wrapped Trojan Magnum condom propped up in front of them. This was clearly no accident. The condom was positioned in such a way that it was absolutely meant to greet me as I entered the room. It was the shining centerpiece of this strategically designed display. Like, it was Ann Miller and the water bottles were a bevy of male dancers perfectly framing it. I don't know if housekeeping was being cute, or someone on staff was trying to make a statement or advances, but there it was.

Perplexed and amused, I called my tour manager to tell him what I'd found, mostly because I just needed someone to share the laugh with me. He was much more unsettled by the whole thing than I was. I told him not to say anything, but of course, he did anyway. Ten minutes later, a hotel manager called up to my room.

"Hello, Mr. Rainbow, this is Ryan, the hotel manager. I understand there was an incident in your room. . . ."

"Not much of an incident," I said in my smiliest voice, hoping to lighten his somber tone. "Just some interesting product placement. No big deal!"

"Could you describe what it was you saw when you entered the room?"

What the hell was this—*Law & Order: Special Victims Unit?*

"Yeah, Ryan, it's a condom."

"I see. . . ." *Scribbling pen noises as he pretends to take notes.*

"No worries," I said, trying to end the call. "Luckily, I have a pretty good sense of humor."

"As the hotel manager, I assure you, I don't find anything funny about this."

"Well, how do you think I feel?" I said. "You didn't even include a man! Hahahahaha!"

Radio silence.

"Would you like me to send someone to retrieve it?" *Because that would make this whole thing less awkward.*

"No, Ryan, that won't be necessary."

"Well, sir, what would you like me to do?"

"Not a thing, Ryan. Thanks for checking in."

The main reason I'm highlighting this particular call from management is to point out a cardinal sin of customer relations that I see has become an epidemic. This would have been a perfect opportunity for Ryan to offer me, let's say, a free-meal voucher or perhaps send up the fucking humidifier that was supposed to be there in the first place. Instead, he chose to pass the burden of resolving this matter to me—an innocent, moderately VIP client with one condom and zero managerial ranking in the hotel he alleges to run.

Ladies and gentlemen of the hospitality and service industries, I implore you to stop asking customers what *they* would like *you* to do. Once you've acknowledged and accepted fault for an incident, it is incumbent on you to then offer a solution. I say this as someone who worked in bars and restaurants for many years. When the establishment I had been hired to represent somehow fell short of its service standard, I did my best to rectify the situation with authority and no prompting by sending a complimentary mac-and-cheese to the customer's table or offering to give them a hand job in the men's room. It's called "professionalism."

The Work

My ninety minutes onstage each night, doing my craft and connecting with my audience while dressed in sequined costumes and bathed in flattering lighting, is a sheer delight. That's pretty much the end of this section.

Okay, let me not be quite so Pollyannaish about it. It takes a lot to get to that stage, and what I've shared so far isn't even half of it. The road is exhausting, and on occasion it can feel tedious doing the same show every night for several months. There are some shows that my tour manager and I affectionately call "chocolate cake" shows. This is in reference to a 2014 Barbra Streisand interview in which she revealed that her mind sometimes wanders while singing her greatest hits in concert and that at times, she might be singing "People" but thinking about what she wants to eat after the show. At one point, she proclaimed, "I might be thinkin' about chocolate cake!" (Barbra, I can feel you.)

The Prostitute (that would be me)

You might assume that life on the road is a revolving door of hotties for an eligible gay bachelor in his prime like *moi*; that I've got a boy toy in every zip code. Well, think again, sweetheart. The sad reality is that I have no social life whatsoever when touring. Why, you ask? Because I was born too soon and started too late—that's why!

Despite what you may think from all that flattering stage lighting and the occasional Instagram filter, I ain't in my twenties anymore. I didn't start touring until I was in my thirties. At the beginning, I experimented with going out after my shows to have a few drinks and check out the local scene. I quickly learned that I could not indulge any of that behavior while also sustaining the energy needed to travel and perform.

Tour life is often lonely, and it can get brutal. I rarely see anything outside my hotel or the theater, and that's really okay with me. (Here's the biggest secret of all about domestic travel: Everywhere in the United States pretty much looks the damn same.) To combat the isolation, I'm often browsing social media and dating apps from my dry, waterless hotel rooms. To date, I've never met any locals in person, but I'm always down for a virtual flirt. Maybe now would be a good time to give you a few pointers on how to break the ice when you see me randomly pop up on your Grindr grid.

Some things that would be nice to say to me on Grindr:

1. *Hello, Randy. Welcome to our fair city. I do hope you enjoy your stay.*

2. *Hey there! Love your work! Have a great day.*

3. *I would like to take you out for a drink. Do let me know if this is of interest. Otherwise, have a great day.*

Some things you should perhaps avoid saying to me on Grindr:

1. *This can't be a real profile. What are you doing here? Is this really you? This has to be fake. I'm reporting you. Is it really you??*

2. *Hey, I recognize you! Here's a picture of my genitals.*

3. *Hey, my mom loves you! Here's a picture of my genitals.*

Allow me to briefly respond to the second list. It's true, there's lots of catfishing going on out there, so I respect your cautious approach. Please also consider that I am just a common whore like the rest of you, and it's not outside the realm of possibility that you might catch me on Grindr from time to time. As for your genitals, I appreciate the generous offering, but I will let you know if and when I am interested in seeing them. I'm a common whore with boundaries and would appreciate a modicum of tact. Thank you for the kind recognition, and feel free to hold on to that poorly lit photograph of your taint. Please also send my best to your mother.

Listen, I don't want you to feel too bad for me. I'm getting indecent proposals right and left out here, and it's not only on Grindr. One time in Atlanta, a married couple (cis man/cis woman) at my meet-and-greet came right out and invited me back to their home for a threesome. The woman told me, very matter-of-factly, that she would like to offer her willing husband to me for the night on the condition that she could watch. How's that for southern hospitality? I thanked them but ultimately declined (even though he was super cute) and asked if they'd settle for a selfie. I do love the ladies, I just don't *love* the ladies, if you know what I'm telling you. Besides, I've always preferred postshow mozzarella sticks to ménages à trois.

The one and only time I ever hooked up with someone from my audience was after a show in New Orleans. A tall, well-built, muscly Dominican man had his picture taken with me and stayed to ask if he could take me out on the town. I knew I had an early flight the next morning, but I said yes, ignoring the better judgment of my tour manager. It was during Mardi Gras, so I don't know if it was all the magic in the air or all the puke on the ground, but I just couldn't resist. (Let's be real—it was all the muscles bulging out of his tank top.) We hopped around to a dozen different bars, making out in every one of them, and eventually wound up back at my hotel room. It felt very *Notting Hill*. We fooled around a bit but didn't go all the way because, ironically, we didn't have any condoms. He should have been at my San Diego show.

The best part of traveling, hands down, is coming home to New York. I spent decades trying to get back here after my parents rudely moved us to South Florida in the '90s without even consulting me. That anyone would make me leave it for any reason now is cruel and unusual, and I resent it. I love this city so much it hurts—almost as much as I sometimes hate it. I know I die a little every day I'm not in it. In fact, I invite all of my fans to come live here, too. Stop making me come to you all the time.

There is, however, always an adjustment period when coming off tour for any amount of time. I give my tour manager shit, but between you and me, it is a fabulous luxury to have someone on-hand at all times to accommodate your every basic need. If I call him at 3 a.m. and tell him I need a loofah sponge and a chocolate Frosty from Wendy's (I would never do that . . . again), he will make it so. It can take a few weeks to come down from that high horse and readapt to civilian life. Sometimes I find myself asking random strangers for Starbucks iced lattes, alas, to no avail. ☹

Diva-complaints aside, it is kind of wonderful to be able to see other parts of this great nation (every once in a while, within reason), and I really do thank God for all the opportunities I'm given. Still, there's no arguing with what Dorothy famously reminds us of at the end of *The Wizard of Oz* (after she gets ditched by the Wizard, and Glinda the good witch is all "Ma'am, what would you like me to do?"): There's no place like home . . . and unless you're in San Diego, don't forget to add condoms to your rider.

9

My Gay Agenda

My fellow Americans, the deep-state media and certain lunatic right-wing groups will have you believe that I have some sort of big, gay plan. A so-called Gay Agenda, if you will. Well, allow me to set the record straight here and now: That is absolutely correct. A Randy Rainbow administration will implement a simple seven-point plan to effectively restore America's fabulousness and officially boots the White House down. It even comes with its own slogan: "Finally, America's Gay Again!" Or, as I like to call it, FAGA.

If you'll just give me a few moments of your time, I will happily walk you through my proposal point-by-point.

Point 1: "Gayer Education"

Now, look . . . some of these nutjobs have accused my community of trying to "groom" their children. Let me tell you something: That is not only sick and offensive, it's also completely illogical. Why would I want to recruit more gay people in this world when it's already damn near impossible to book a brunch reservation in Manhattan on a Sunday? Honestly, people, use your heads.

That said, under my administration, all public schools will adhere to a strict dress code that will include uniforms designed and hand-sequined by Emmy and Tony Award–winner Bob Mackie, stiletto slingback pumps (no lower than five inches), a fully beat face with a bold lip, and mandatory lashes.

Some leaders have taken steps to ban certain books from our school libraries, which is absurd. As president, I will ban all books except those written by me, Jacqueline Susann, Martha Stewart, and Alan Cumming. I promise to replace them with back issues of *Cosmo*, *Vogue* (the André Leon Talley years only . . . sorry, Anna), the *Advocate*, and *Mandate*.

Jazz, tap, and ballet will replace all other physical education, including extracurricular sports. Teachers will be encouraged to devote more of their lesson plans to the history of American pop culture and less to American history. It's staggering how much of our country's youth can recite the Gettysburg Address but can't quote even one of Olympia Dukakis's lines from *Steel Magnolias* or re-create the iconic "Jingle Bell Rock" dance sequence from *Mean Girls*.

Other antiquated subjects like math and science will no longer be prioritized over the most fundamental building blocks of a well-rounded education, like Barbra, Judy, and RuPaul's Critical Drag Race Theory.

Point 2: "The Supreme Court, She Is Packing"

This unhinged Supreme Court is trying to dismantle our rights, one by one. That is why I plan to pack the damn thing tighter than Jon Hamm in a pair of slim-fit chinos. And not with just any ol' progressives. By executive order, and with the help of a congressional majority (whatever that means), for every radically conservative justice, I will install one bad-bitch drag queen to counter his or her destruction. Let's make the courts WERK for the people once and for all, America! Here are just a few sample appointments:

- With his questionable past and erratic temperament, I fear nobody's safe with Brett Kavanaugh around. So I'm pairing him with another dangerous queen. That's right . . . say hello to Justice Bianca Del Rio! (Not today, Kavanaugh.)

- Clarence Thomas is so full of shit, the toilet is jealous. And talk about a problematic past . . . he makes Brett Kavanaugh look like Little Orphan Annie. Luckily for us, he'll be getting just the tucking he needs from his brand-new work wife, Justice Jinkx Monsoon.

- Hey, Gummie Beary Carrots or Amy Coney Barrett or whatever your name is . . . honey, you bring the drama, but this ain't *Maury Povich*! Meet your worst nightmare and my newest appointee . . . Justice Trixie Mattel!

- I can't wait to dilute Neil Gorsuch's power, and I know just the icon for the job. Haaaaay, Justice Bob the Drag Queen . . . you up, gurl? (Good luck, Neil Gor-suck.)

Point 3: "My Hottie, My Choice!"

Voting is a cornerstone of democracy and the fundamental right of all American citizens. Sadly, that right continues to be endangered due to ongoing voter suppression, which has been on the rise for decades. And politics is just the tip of the iceberg. These nefarious efforts to silence the voice of the people have historically led to unfair outcomes in many of our most consequential races. Like Angela Bassett's shocking loss of the best actress Academy Award for *What's Love Got to Do with It?*, Dixie Carter not even once (yes, you read that correctly) being Emmy-nominated for *Designing Women*, Beck stealing the 2015 best album Grammy from Beyoncé, Jake Gyllenhaal not only losing the Oscar for *Brokeback Mountain* but also being snubbed by the Golden Globes, Greta Gerwig not being nominated as best director for *Barbie*, and don't even get me started on the famous *Yentl* Awards Season Massacre of 1983.

Under my administration, these important contests will no longer be decided by elitist committees like the Electoral College and the Academy of Motion Pictures Arts and Sciences. Once elected, I will immediately sign into law a brand-new federal statute I'm calling the Disgruntled Margot Robbie Act (or DMRA). This landmark legislation will rightfully place all critical decision-making back in the hands of you, the people, by enabling you to easily vote *American Idol*–style via text for your chosen nominees across all categories, political and otherwise. (Standard messaging and data rates may apply.)

Point 4: "Really, Lindsey Graham?"

That one is self-explanatory.

Point 5: "Let's Get Rock-Hard on Infrastructure"

I think we can all agree that there's nothing more depressing than a soft infrastructure. And right now, America's crumbling foundation is limper than Pete Buttigieg at a Hooters in Wyoming. So I'm prepared to introduce a brand-new bipartisan infrastructure deal that, trust me, will be totally gay-partisan by the time I'm through with it.

Under the fierce supervision of my secretary of interior design, celebrity decorator Nate Berkus, our highly qualified design squad, led by Joanna Gaines from HGTV's hit show *Fixer Upper* and *Queer Eye*'s Bobby Berk, will give this country the full glam makeover she so desperately needs. We'll start by ripping up all those unsightly asphalt highways and airplane runways and replacing them with rich walnut prime-grade hardwood flooring. The tacky old steel tunnels and railways of yesterseason will be redone in exposed brick and gorgeous distressed shiplap paneling to retain their vintage feel. It'll be "rustic 1930s cottage cozy-chic and midcentury modern Americana with a classic colonial twist," but, like, still super infrastructury.

It remains vitally important that all Americans have suitable access to hair care. That's why I've budgeted $6 billion to install thousands of conveniently placed blowout stations across the country, equipped with an array of only the finest styling products. Equinox+Starbucks fitness coffee combos will be erected (lol) at every major intersection, while nonessential buildings like certain banks, hospitals, and national landmarks will be replaced by Sephora supercenters. Honey, it's time to bedazzle these bridges and sissy these sidewalks until we are snatched to our core assets.

Point 6: "Pride Cometh Before the Summer"

It warms my heart to see so many out-and-proud members of the LGBTQIA+++Broccoli emoji community living their best lives each June. But with such a diverse and ever-expanding group, I really think we need a little more time to celebrate. So, starting in my first term, Pride month will begin in March and run all the way through September. Of course, I know what many of you are thinking: Won't that interfere with other major holidays like Easter and Independence Day? Those will be canceled.

Point 7: "Take a Stand . . . Rebrand"

As your new "Rebrander-in-Chief," and something of a marketing expert myself, I know there's nothing middle America loves more than queer merch. Hear me out: I'm talking Dylan Mulvaney on every can from Bud Light to Goya beans, shirtless Lil Nas X on every Starbucks Christmas cup, and the new face of NASCAR . . . Paul Lynde.

Of course, that's only the start. We really need to gay things up around here, and I'm thinking big picture. Within my first one hundred days, we will quadruple the number of Pride flags on display and officially *zhuzh* all major national monuments. Move over, Lady Liberty! We've loved your work, but it's high time we made a new Lady our mascot, and her name is Gaga. I have already commissioned a 350-foot faux gold–plated statue of Stefani Joanne Angelina Germanotta, and trust that she will slay the Harbor, henny! Mount Rushmore will also be freshly carved to include other gay icons such as Liza Minnelli, Kylie Minogue, Cher, and Matt Bomer.

To ensure an effective rollout of my Gay Agenda, every US citizen will receive a stimulus package including a FAGA baseball cap, a pair of my signature Pink Glasses, a $200 Gucci gift card, and a bonus box set of Dolly Parton's greatest hits.

10

I Feel Bad About My Balls

Did you know that I am supposed to have the body of actor Jacob Elordi? It's true. In case you're misinterpreting that, allow me to explain before Mr. Elordi's legal team goes petitioning for a restraining order.

You see, I was supposed to have been born with the six-foot-three-inch, lean, muscular physique currently inhabited by Australian heartthrob and *Euphoria* star Jacob Elordi. Jacob Elordi has a long, chiseled torso that stretches endlessly betwixt his broad, angular shoulders and trim, thirty-inch waist. He has perky pecs that perfectly align with his sculpted, muscular arms and six-pack abs that end in those coveted V-lines above his pelvic region that you see only on Ken dolls and people with four percent body fat. His ass appears to have been carved by Michelangelo, and his thick, meaty legs go on for about a mile-and-a-half. I do not have those things.

Jacob Elordi can wear absolutely anything and make it look like a designer's wet dream. He could throw on an old Hanes T-shirt and a pair of torn denim shorts, walk a red carpet, and look as though he were rocking the latest couture fashion. I, on the other hand, would be quickly escorted off the red carpet for wearing the same. This, however, is not my fault. I am fairly confident that I am the victim of a cosmic error that wrongly assigned me to my body and not that of Jacob Elordi.

I learned this logic from my grandmother, who used to make similar observations. She'd spot a tall, blond, statuesque woman with voluptuous curves and a killer rack walking through the mall and say, "See? That's the body I'm supposed to have," as though she had ordered a chocolate ice-cream cone and somebody accidentally gave her pistachio. This was merely an amusing running joke, but I also found it to be a useful psychological mechanism. It can lighten the burden of body envy and alleviate body self-shaming by transferring the blame to another, imaginary entity: *Well, I'm supposed to have a six-pack, but somebody somewhere obviously made a mistake.*

Of course, this could also be interpreted as a cop-out since we annoyingly do bear at least some responsibility for our own physical forms. I guess I could look slightly more like Jacob Elordi if I spent more time at the gym instead of just watching other people working out on Instagram, which is currently my fitness program. The thing is, I suffer from a medical condition that prevents me from working out more intensively: I don't wanna. And let's face it, there are certain genetic limitations that also hinder my ability to appear shirtless on the cover of GQ (not to mention the fact that they haven't asked). Even if I worked out nine days a week, I still would not look like Jacob Elordi.

Now, listen, I don't want to be too self-deprecating here. I'm still on the market, after all. And I can still command a price, if you know what I'm saying. I think I'm pretty cute, as a matter of fact, and I receive my fair share of romantic interest from others — particularly sexually confused men and middle-aged women in Atlanta (see chapter about touring). Still, despite what I would consider a moderate supply of self-confidence, I do not have the perfect proportions of a Jacob fucking Elordi. I never will, and for that, I take serious issue with whoever is responsible.

I am what I believe is referred to in the body industry as "an apple." I have a shorter, rounder torso with long, skinny limbs. Isn't that just great? I have dainty, frail wrists that make it impossible for me to wear watches or bracelets lest I evoke memories of Bea Arthur in her later years. I cannot gain muscle or fat in my arms or legs. It's simply impossible. I believe my arms and legs are under some sort of legal obligation to remain the same size they have been since my bar mitzvah. This is also true of my very modest ass, which is really more the somewhat anticlimactic dénouement to my lower back than its own feature presentation. Despite my best efforts, any weight I put on goes defiantly to my face and midsection. Thanks to my relentless body dysmorphia (as well, I fear, as a certain amount of stubborn reality), this often has me seeing the Kool-Aid Man when I stare at my naked reflection in the mirror—or, more specifically, someone wearing a Kool-Aid Man Halloween costume in a listing on Amazon. Aside from all those things, I feel terrific!

I, like so many, have struggled with food and body issues since my childhood. I touched a bit on the topic of my eating disorder in my first book but realize I left it kind of open-ended. I never neatly wrapped up that part of my story. So here, finally, is the great conclusion you've all been waiting for: It never ends. My journey toward achieving a perfectly healthy relationship with food and body image remains ongoing. The good news is, it seems to have gotten much better for me over the years in that I have developed skills to effectively manage and navigate it.

Age can be a great friend. It makes you wiser and less fearful of a lot of things. It's also not for sissies, as Bette Davis famously said. Unfortunately, "sissy" is exactly how I identify. Bette Davis wasn't even a gay man (technically), so gurl didn't know the half of it! That said, I actually think I have a pretty good attitude about age these days. People are living longer and staying hotter well into their later years, and we need to recalibrate the way we think of age numerically. The definitions we assign to our years are ever-changing. We have to recognize that and start embracing age without fear or shame. Still, even though I'm currently only fort—thirty-sev—THIRTY-SIX YEARS OLD, I am beginning to notice some of nature's, shall we say, unwelcome developments.

I feel bad about my balls. Truly I do. By that I mean I am concerned that they are not quite in the same place they once were. Don't be too concerned. I don't mean they're in Bulgaria or anything. My balls have not been kidnapped. Oh, God, is that what you thought? No, I just mean that they might be a little lower than they were ten to fifteen years ago. I can't say for sure, but I kind of feel like they are, and it makes me sad. Maybe sad isn't what I feel about it. I guess it makes me nervous. What's next?

If you saw my balls, you'd probably say something polite like "I don't know what you're talking about . . . your balls are fine! They look like perfectly normal, healthy balls. They're adorable, even!" Then again, you might just say, "Sir, why are you showing me your balls?" These would all be fair arguments.

To be clear, they're not touching water when I sit down or anything. Oh, God, is that what you thought? I've heard those horror stories, though, and I'm relieved (and a bit puffed up) to report that I'm not quite there yet. Still, I do notice a subtle difference, and I don't like it. You may consider this a silly and superficial concern, and I totally hear you. I guess you have to try to put it in perspective. See, I don't have children. I am not reminded of the slipping sands of time by milestones like birthdays, graduations, or teen pregnancies. I have only my balls. For all intents and purposes, my balls are like my children. I feel like you still don't get it.

This latest development is only one—well, I guess technically two—of the changes I'm beginning to notice. I feel a few new aches and pains and hear some extra cracks and crunches when I get out of bed in the morning. That could be from all the traveling I do for work, but maybe it's not. And in the grand tradition of good ol' metabolisms, mine ain't what she used to be. My weight is constantly in flux. Here, I'll demonstrate in real time: Right now, I weigh 152 pounds, but since the mere mention of food causes me to go up a dress size, check in with me again at the end of the next paragraph.

I'm also much more affected, physically and emotionally, by my diet. I can't recklessly binge certain foods or alcoholic beverages like I once did without severely impacting my mood. I can still put down an entire medium-sized mushroom-and-pepperoni pizza (by which I mean a large) in one sitting, but not without committing a felony the next morning—perhaps murder. Then I eat some flaxseeds and I'm Mary-freaking-Poppins. FYI, I now weigh 159 pounds.

Back to my balls. I looked it up, and there's a procedure called a scrotal lift. There's an office on the Upper West Side, not far from my apartment, that does them. I'm not saying I'm quite ready for that yet, but I did just bookmark the page. It says it's an outpatient surgery that firms and tightens the area, giving a more youthful appearance. I don't know. Maybe I'll just get hair extensions down there or something.

I must say, I am all for plastic surgery. I haven't had any myself yet, but I do hope to one day. Well, I guess I kind of just lied to you. I did undergo a cosmetic procedure once, but it's not what you may think. (Wait . . . what are you thinking?) I haven't had any rhinoplasties or chin implants. In fact, I haven't done anything even minimally invasive above the neck, not even Botox or any of those facial resurfacing laser treatments. I look forward to dipping my toe in those ponds very soon, but I guess

I'm kind of a late bloomer. I'm embarrassed to admit that it was only last year that I got my first facial. I am, however, very serious about skin care. I've been moisturizing like a crazy person since I was eighteen. I spend a lot of money on what I believe to be the finest products, and the bulk of my days is spent cleansing, exfoliating, toning, seruming, and hydrating. It's a wonder I even have time to write this book. You know that Alfred Hitchcock thriller called *The 39 Steps*? That was actually based on my daily skin-care regimen.

To date, my one and only experience with cosmetic surgery was in 2005, when I got what I affectionately refer to as my boob job. More specifically, I had liposuction to remove some over-developed breast tissue in my chest caused by a fairly common condition known as gynecomastia. For those who don't know, this sometimes occurs in boys going through puberty and can be quite psychologically and socially distressing. In fact, my palms are sweating just thinking about it. It's funny—I haven't really thought about this much in almost twenty years. Most of my closest friends don't even know about it, but it caused me so much mental anguish in my childhood and into my young adulthood that even writing about it now gets me a little *fak-lempt*.

I was that little fat kid at the neighborhood swimming pool wearing a T-shirt in the water. This, on its own, often led to taunts, jeers, and confused stares from other kids and their parents, but I was sure it would be nothing compared to what they'd say or think if they saw what I was hiding underneath. I was bullied relentlessly at school, and of course, my weight was the most popular point of criticism for schoolyard bullies. (Schoolyard bullies rarely attack one's politics.) This led to severe depression and self-hatred, which led to more eating, which led to more bullying, and you get the picture. I often felt trapped in my own body and didn't know how to escape. At best, this inevitably sharpened my skills of deflection through humor and taught me how to accessorize with scarves and dress up my T-shirts with cute vests in order to camouflage my unwanted curves. (Oh, I went through a serious vest phase.) At worst, it sometimes left me in tears, locked in a bathroom at home for hours, punching myself in my bare chest and abdomen to the point of painful bruising. By the time I turned nineteen, I had devoted myself to fitness and eventually got in much better shape, but it was never perfect. It is never perfect.

A few years later, I was working at a restaurant in Manhattan where I met and fell madly in love with a boy. He was a server named Adam, and he was magical. He was tall and muscular with big brown puppy-dog eyes and a goatee, and he laughed genuinely at all my jokes. He was twenty-four, but he looked forty-eight. He was also bowlegged, which, for whatever reason, is a deformity I have always found extremely attractive in men. He was an artistic type with a quiet warmth about him, but he also had a bit of a rough, brutish exterior—sort of a young, gay Bill Sikes type, for any *Oliver Twist* fans out there. He often said whatever popped into his head without thinking first. It was usually very endearing.

One year at the restaurant's annual Christmas party, Adam and I had a few too many Jägermeister shots (exactly the right amount of too many) and wound up making out in a bathroom stall before throwing up in unison on West Eighth Street. It was a real holiday romance. From that night on, we were the hot topic and subject of much gossip and speculation among our coworkers. Nothing physical had really transpired beyond our Christmas make-out sesh, but there was now definitely a more palpable flirtation between us during our shared shifts.

I started working out a lot more, which is typical when I'm

feeling generally positive about things. If Adam and I were going to go any further, I wanted to be ready to impress him. I figured this would be a good time to finally lose some of my residual baby fat. I even started working out with a trainer. I was using muscles, including my pectoral muscles, in ways I never had before. I felt great, but after a few weeks, much to my shock and concern, I noticed that the pesky fatty tissue in that region was not disappearing but instead was protruding more prominently thanks to the muscle I had built up underneath. I had not felt self-conscious about this in years, and suddenly here I was again. This was not good.

Hoping I was the only one who might notice, I decided I would try to ignore it and go about my business. Even if someone did notice it a little, who cared? I was an adult now, after all. I was in the real world, not the schoolyard, and therefore would no longer have to contend with schoolyard bullies. (Of all the lies my mother told me, I think that one's still my favorite.) So that's just what I did—I went about my business. And when I arrived at work one day in a slightly clingy V-neck cashmere-blend sweater from H&M, Adam said the first thing that popped into his head without thinking first: "Hey, bitch-tits!"

For those not familiar, *bitch-tits* is the decidedly nonmedical locker-room term for gynecomastia, perhaps more vulgar and offensive than its other, slightly more widely known street slang counterparts, such as *man boobs*—or *moobs* if you're trying to save some time. It's also what I originally wanted to title this book: *Bitch-Tits: The Randy Rainbow Story.* That idea was strongly discouraged by my publisher.

After this gut punch from Adam, whom I fell out of love with in that moment and who likely did not realize the gravity of his comment, I quickly regressed to my teenage self. My now robust social life had paused indefinitely. I was canceling plans right and left and sometimes even calling out of work. This spike in shame suddenly made going out for groceries feel like an existential threat on my worst days. On the days I did go to work, I had developed a new system of taping my chest down with masking tape, which irritated my skin terribly and is not recommended. I was desperate and didn't know what else to do.

In my desperation, for the first time ever, I started researching surgical options. I made a list of offices that offered this procedure, most of which were on Manhattan's Upper East Side, and booked a few consultations. This was notably a huge step for me, not only because it was the most aggressively proactive I had ever been about this fatty-tissue issue that had haunted me since childhood but because I had always been freaked out by the idea of any kind of surgery. Knives and needles just ain't my thing. I had never even had stitches before. Okay, that's kind of a lie, too.

There was this one time when I was eleven . . . I was home alone one afternoon, fixing my favorite after-school snack: a toasted everything bagel with egg salad. (I didn't make the egg salad myself; it was premade by Mom and left in a Tupperware container in the fridge. What do you think, I was some kind of culinary prodigy?) I grabbed the largest bread knife I could find and began slicing with wild abandon, totally disregarding proper bagel-slicing technique: I held the bagel upright with my left hand on one side and aimed the tip of the knife in my right hand directly at the left hand holding the bagel. You know where this is going. I got to about the center of the bagel and the knife pierced right through that tender, fleshy part of the hand between the thumb and index finger (I just googled, and I believe it's called the thenar web space). There was so much blood that our kitchen looked like a crime scene. My mother had to rush home from work and drive me to the ER, where I received three entire stitches. I can glance down as I write this now and still see the tiny scar: a shameful, permanent memorial to the Jewiest war wound ever self-inflicted by an eleven-year-old.

Children, I'm sure this book has been banned in your school libraries by now, but in case you're seeing this, allow me this teachable moment to remind you of the proper way to safely slice a bagel:

1. Place the bagel flat on an appropriate cutting surface with your nondominant hand resting on top. Using a serrated bread knife in your dominant hand, place the blade parallel to your cutting surface and cut horizontally, lightly applying pressure with your nondominant hand to secure the bagel.

2. Once halfway through (this is very important!), stand the bagel up on its side and move your nondominant hand to the top of the bagel. Continue cutting in a downward motion toward the cutting surface and away from your hand, obviously!

This concludes the bagel-cutting PSA portion of this chapter. Now, back to my moobs . . .

After a few meetings, I found a doctor I liked. The consultation form he sent me home with said the surgery would cost $6,000. I was twenty-three with barely a dime to my name, so I called my favorite egg-salad maker and launched an impassioned pitch for some financial aid. Thankfully, she didn't take much convincing. My mother knew how important this was to me, and ultimately, she and my father agreed to foot the bill. Mom flew up from Florida to be with me on the day of the surgery. I was a nervous wreck. I heard my mother threatening the surgeon and nurses as they brought me into the operating room: "I only got one kid—be careful with him!" After that, I remember being asked to count backwards from one hundred. I got to about ninety-eight, and the next thing I knew, I heard a nurse saying, "All done! Flat as a pancake!" And I was. A few weeks later, I removed the compression vest, put on that clingy V-neck cashmere sweater from H&M, looked at myself in the mirror, and cried happy tears.

That was my first and only experience with cosmetic surgery . . . so far. . . .

I would like to make an announcement: I will not be aging gracefully. I constantly hear people bragging that they will. These people are obnoxious. They say things like "I love my wrinkles" and "I can't wait to see the story my face tells when I'm older." Shut up. God willing, if all goes according to plan, the only story my older face will be telling is a lie: that it's twenty years younger. My face will lie so much, they're going to start fact-checking it on CNN. It might even say things like "I sleep eight hours every night" and "I've never touched an alcoholic beverage." Don't ask questions. Just believe everything it says.

Ladies and gentlemen, please be forewarned that when the moment inevitably comes that Father Time darkens my doorstep and starts knocking too loudly for me to ignore, I plan to nip and tuck and lift and suck until I am back in the womb. I may wind up looking like a science experiment and be unable to convey raw emotion, but dammit, my face will only tell the story of a high-society kween who's done well enough in life to spend every other weekend at Dr. Schwartzbaum's office on Madison and East Seventy-Seventh.

Of course, I know the social risks involved. We've all seen the red-carpet photos of botched face jobs that have left some of Hollywood's most famous celebrities looking unrecognizable. What's worse, these poor, aging A-listers, hoping to cling to a little dignity and professional viability, fall prey to the evil trolls who comment mercilessly on their altered appearance. To this point, I have taken the liberty of having my lawyer draw up the following agreement for my friends, family, fans, followers, and anyone reading this book. Please review it at your leisure and sign below where indicated.

THIS PROFESSIONAL AND VERY SERIOUS AGREEMENT IS MADE AND ENTERED INTO AS OF IMMEDIATELY BY AND BETWEEN RANDY RAINBOW (THE "FAMOUS CELEBRITY") AND THE WORLD.

WHEREAS, Randy Rainbow wishes to reserve all rights to maintain his youthful and vibrant appearance by any artificial and/or unconventional means necessary, without interference or unflattering analysis by his friends, family, fans, or followers (the "Peanut Gallery"); and

WHEREAS, the Peanut Gallery will agree not to comment negatively in any way on the result of any such artificial or unconventional means;

THEREFORE, in consideration of the foregoing, the parties, intending to be legally bound, hereby agree to the following:

1.   Should Randy Rainbow do anything weird to his face, including but not limited to receiving excessive amounts of injectable fillers, leaving said face swollen and generally unfamiliar, the Peanut Gallery agrees to not make known, by use of catty remarks or feigned genuine concern, suspicions of any such enhancements. The Peanut Gallery will instead agree to assume that Randy Rainbow simply had an especially restful night or is experiencing the natural glow of collagen supplements prescribed to him by Jennifer Aniston.

2.   Regarding any undeniable and/or shocking bodily augmentations, including but not limited to cosmetic rib removal, fat transference, liposuction, and buttock implantations, the Peanut

Gallery agrees henceforth to shut the fuck up, with the exception of any contrived flattery or acknowledgment of Randy Rainbow's commendable commitment to health and fitness.

3. Should Randy Rainbow overtly dye his hair at the first noticeable sign of grayness, resulting in a questionable appearance or said hair dye dripping in a disgusting manner down his face while in a public forum, the signatory of this agreement swears to in no way mock or satirize Randy Rainbow on social media or any such platform, as Randy Rainbow has frequently done regarding other public figures who will herein remain nameless.

4. In the likely event of a full, Liberace-level facelift occurring roughly thirty years from the creation of this document and resulting in Randy Rainbow's inability to blink or hold liquids in his mouth, the Peanut Gallery will not question or acknowledge any of the disturbing indications of drastic facial modification described herein but instead concede that no time has passed since 2008.

This agreement has been duly executed by the authorized representatives of the parties hereto, forthwith, backforth, step, kick, kick, leap, kick, touch, shuffle ball change, as of immediately and forevermore as long as you both shall live, amen.

Randy Rainbow
_____
Randy Rainbow, the "Famous Celebrity"

_____
The Peanut Gallery (PLEASE SIGN HERE)

Okay, fine, maybe I'm being a little overdramatic. (I would still like you to sign, though.) In reality, I have every intention of being judicious—conservative, even—about any of my possible future plastic surgeries, and I recommend the same to anyone who's interested in my opinion. Let me be clear: I am by no means a qualified professional and have almost no personal experience in this field. By today's standards, that makes me an expert, and so you should listen to everything I say. While I am a major proponent of people doing anything that might make them look or feel better about themselves (within reason), I do think it's advisable when considering any kind of permanent cosmetic enhancements to start small, build gradually, and not go overboard. That's why I plan to begin with some light microdermabrasion, perhaps followed by a little Botox around the eye area, and progress sensibly toward having my entire head permanently grafted onto Jacob Elordi's body.

I must say, it feels good to talk about this stuff. It deserves notice that I seem to have reached a point in life where, for all the old insecurities I still fight, I feel comfortable and confident enough to talk—even joke—about topics the likes of scrotal nostalgia, my lipo (which for many years I wouldn't even admit to those closest to me), and, most embarrassing of all, the infamous bagel disaster of 1992. It's all out in the open now, and I'm glad it's there. As the saying goes (I think): We're only as sick as our suctions.

I guess one really great thing about age is the courage it can bring. Another thing I've heard people say on the subject is that you stop sweating the small stuff, and even the big, bad wolves you once feared turn out to be not so big and bad after all. My rocky relationship with my body image has traveled a long and winding road that may never end, but I'm glad it's at least gotten me to this latest chapter, which I'm proudly calling my "Nora Ephron moment." I wonder if Tom Hanks and Meg Ryan will be available for the rom-com film adaptation: *You've Got Bitch-Tits*.

11

Life Sucks, Wear the Damn Lipstick

I love makeup! I just think it's terrific. I'm so grateful for makeup. I love everything it gives us: the confidence, the glamour, even the occasional adult acne. I'm always wearing it, at least to some extent. I'll never forget the time, several years ago, when a manager at the Manhattan gay bar where I was working told me while punching in a drink order that he would never even go downstairs to his own mailbox without at least a little foundation and brow pencil. It changed my whole philosophy of life.

Don't get it twisted, now. My cosmetological skills in no way rival or even come close to those of modern-day drag artists. And I cannot hold a Real Techniques Ultra Plush Blush Makeup Brush to the sorcery of some of these new beauty influencers who can change the world with waterproof mascara and cure cancer by contouring. Believe it or not, I'm more a "basic color-correcting, sensibly bronzed, moderately to slightly more prominently sparkly on occasion" kind of makeup gay. In other words, I like to have that nice, healthy, pregnant glow, but I'm rarely serving false lashes and a smoky eye.

Even though I don't consider myself a pro, many people ask me for makeup tips and what brands I use. Many of my followers (a word I hate because it sounds super culty, but "fans" sounds too pretentious, and I want you to like me) have even requested that

I include a chapter on the subject in my next book, which is this, so here we are. Truth be told, I used to be exclusively MAC all the way until I recently found out that it's Donald Jessica Trump's preferred brand. Needless to say, it's been a really challenging time for me. Anyway, half the fun is experimenting with different brands, and there are so many I love, like Estée Lauder, NARS, Rare Beauty, Fenty Beauty, Clinique, Pat McGrath, Dior, Bobbi Brown, Tarte. . . . My editor thinks that listing all of these brand names is a cheap ploy to meet my word count for this book. What he fails to realize is that it's actually a cheap ploy to score an endorsement deal, or at least some free swag.

I can watch a makeup tutorial for hours on end without ever getting bored and always learn something new and constructive. There's a lot of horror in the world right now, and I often wish I could teleport myself to another time in history, but one thing I'm jazzed about is this inclusive beauty revolution we're currently in. People of all genders and ages seem to be feeling a new freedom to express themselves however the hell they want. It's inspiring. Everyone's looking good, feeling good, and having a little fun, and I am so here for it.

That said, I do take issue with the slew of rambunctious teenagers suddenly gallivanting about my local Sephora after school while I'm trying to get through my weekly shopping list. I absolutely blame TikTok for this. While I encourage cosmetic inclusivity, there must be boundaries. Parents, please handle your offspring. Your thirteen-year-old daughters do not need anti-aging serum, and your adolescent sons should be at home after school, stealing their makeup from their mothers' medicine cabinets like real men.

I had my first experiences wearing stage makeup at an early age. I was placed in ballet lessons when I was six, and every dance recital or annual main-stage production of *The Nutcracker* was another opportunity to be lightly made up by the studio's resident "makeup artist." The dance studio was on Long Island, where we lived at the time, in the late 1980s, and this woman was straight out of central casting: massive auburn bouffant, lots of clanky plastic jewelry, loud animal prints . . . major Peg Bundy vibes. One of her favorite hobbies was pluralizing words for no good reason. I remember feeling terrified that her egregious, foot-long acrylic nails might decapitate me as she hurriedly wiped base all over me and patted a touch of pink lipstick on my cheeks and mouth. A variation of the same "consultation" would take place every time.

"Oh, we gotta give you some pigmentations, honey. Yaw lips ah so pale," she'd sing in a thick Long Island accent.

"They are?" I'd ask, distressed by the news and squinting through one half-opened eye to avoid being permanently blinded by a Clairol-coated Ginsu knife.

"Yeah, ya got no cuh-luh!" (Translation: "You have no color.") "Maybe you're anemic or somethin'."

"What does that mean?"

"I don't know, like, ya don't got enough eye-uhn in ya hemo-globins." (Translation: "You may not have enough iron in your hemoglobin.")

"My what-goblins?"

"Like, red blood cells or somethin'. Just go home and tell ya muthah to give ya a hamburgah."

Though grateful for the astute medical advice, I was always much more concerned with her comments about my coloring. This led to a years-long quest for that perfect pop of color that had always eluded me, and hours of self-consciously staring in mirrors while pinching my lips, trying to get some blood flow in that region. I believe that if I were that same age today, I would probably be marching around with a bold mauve Rihanna-inspired lip and a high gloss. But back in the late 1900s, we queer kids had to be more resourceful.

A few years later, when I was about eleven and living with my parents in South Florida, I made a friend at school named Katy. She was petite with fiery red hair, pointy eyebrows, and even more freckles than I had. She looked like an adorable, evil strawberry. Katy had an exceptional singing voice and a very pushy stage mother. She was always going on auditions and had recently landed the title role in a regional theater production of *Annie*. As South Floridian eleven-year-olds go, this chick was booked and busy—a real showbiz pro. We used to harmonize with each other on our favorite pop and musical theater standards, and Katy would always make fun of the way my forehead bobbed up and down in rhythm with my vibrato. She was talented, mean, and scary, and she made me feel bad about myself, so naturally I developed a romantic interest. I asked her if she would "go out with me" (the sixth-grade equivalent of a marriage proposal), and she accepted.

We were both latchkey kids and wound up back at her house one day after school. Her parents and siblings were not home, so we found ourselves all alone. Katy took me upstairs (a clear violation of her mother's rules when she was not present), and something happened that would change my life forever. There, on the thick-beige-carpeted floor of her otherwise bright yellow bedroom . . . Katy showed me her makeup Caboodle.

For those unfamiliar, Caboodles were wildly popular, brightly colored, typically two-toned makeup cases that dominated the beauty organization scene in the '90s. Every girl had one, and though I had heard the term before, this was my first time actually witnessing its plastic majesty in person. Katy's Caboodle organizer was solid teal blue on top and purple jelly sparkle on the bottom. It was sparsely embellished with only a few strategically placed puffy stickers ranging in genre from officially licensed Care Bears to more generic hearts, flowers, and smiley faces. Clearly, Katy had taken a decidedly minimalistic approach to her Caboodle so as to lend a personalized flare without interrupting the natural beauty of its sleek and stylish design.

My palms were sweating as Katy unfastened the circular neon pink latch adorned with random multicolored Tetris shapes, producing a perfect ASMR-inducing click that made me tingle in my high-waisted green-and-black Lycra biker shorts. As she lifted the handle and pulled back the lid, a bright light suddenly beamed out of the case like the sun's rays, creating a warm golden glow that filled the room. If I remember correctly, a kaleidoscope of animated Lisa Frank butterflies fluttered out and up toward the ceiling, bursting into a shimmering cloud of pink-and-silver sparkles that softly rained down on us.

I gazed down past the built-in makeup mirror into the contents of the case and gasped in astonishment. A single tear rolled down my cheek. There, pristinely arranged in the purple jelly compartments, were seemingly endless tubes of Wet n Wild lipstick, blushes, powders, pencils and potions, roll-on glitter sticks, iridescent hair clips, super-control gel, a tube of Dream perfume by GAP Scents, endless Lip Smackers lip glosses in flavors ranging from bubblegum to watermelon, and bottles of Hard Candy nail polish in every shade imaginable. Suddenly, the whole room smelled like Tiffani-Amber Thiessen. I asked Katy how she even knew to buy all this stuff.

"I'm a girl, idiot," she snapped back. A rush of shame washed over me. I was so into her.

Katy grabbed a scrunchie from the Caboodle, and just as she was about to close the lid and push it back under her bed, we heard her mother's car pull into the driveway. She darted downstairs, screaming for me to follow her before the front door opened. In a moment of weakness and confused frenzy, I randomly snatched the first two items I could from the case: a bottle of red nail polish and a green-apple Lip Smacker. Terrified that she might turn around, I followed Katy downstairs, shoving the loot into my shirt pocket before she could notice.

I used up the Lip Smacker almost instantly (that shit was delicious) and kept the nail polish hidden in the back of my closet along with my sexuality for years, long after Katy and I had broken up. (Translation: "long after we had stopped awkwardly holding hands in the cafeteria and asking our moms to drive us to the mall on weekends.") I'd take the Hard Candy bottle out from time to time, just to study it alone in my room, but never had the guts to try it on.

Ironically, I was always unabashedly pushing gender boundaries in other ways as a kid, dressing up in costumes and makeshift wigs to pretend I was my favorite female characters from stage and screen. That kind of theatrical pageantry was not something I normally hid from my parents. Although, actually, I'm just now remembering that I used to sneak into my mom's closet before she got home from work and try on her high heels. She won't learn of that until she reads this, and I'm sure she'll be more surprised by the fact that she ever wore high heels.

Unsurprisingly, the men in our family were less comfortable with my drag tendencies. To be honest, I always secretly delighted in confusing the shit out of my father. I, of course, had a great affinity for musicals and the golden age of Hollywood, always play-acting and quoting old movies. I also had a thing for made-for-TV miniseries. I remember, when I was about twelve, obsessing over one called *Scarlett* based on the 1991 novel that was a sequel to *Gone with the Wind*, starring Joanne Whalley as Scarlett O'Hara. For two weeks, I walked around our house clacking a lace-trimmed folding fan my grandmother had given me and saying, "Jumpin' Jehoshaphat!" and "Fiddle-dee-dee!" to everything. Once my father walked into the living room and found me strutting back and forth with a silk scarf on my head, wearing my mom's wool winter gloves and twirling a Minnie Mouse parasol.

"What are you supposed to be?" he asked solemnly.

Quoting a line from the trailer I'd seen for that night's upcoming episode, with overcooked southern belle melodrama, I said defiantly, "I am a woman of considerable means!"

He stared out the window for a few seconds, then turned around and walked back out of the room.

I finally worked up the nerve to crack open that bottle of Hard Candy nail polish one day. "It's just a clump of hard, dead skin cells," I told myself, staring at my bare fingernail, cursing social constructionism and trying to fan the sudden flame of bravery I felt coming on. "What's the big deal if I want to dress it up a little?" I was indignant. I allowed myself to paint my two index fingers only. That way, if any school bullies gave me shit (a common occurrence in those days), I could tuck them under my thumbs. Middle schoolers back then were not as forward-thinking as they are today. Inevitably, one of the jocks caught a glimpse of me in the hallway.

"Ooooh, how pretty," he said, pushing me up against the wall. "What color is that, fairy?"

In my panic, I blurted out the first thing that came to mind: a line from the 1939 film *The Women*.

"Jungle Red," I said in my best Rosalind Russell. "Isn't it divine?!"

He was so confused that he let me go and kept walking. That was good enough for me.

As an adult, I now wear nail polish proudly and often, on every finger. It brings me simple joy, and I do it for the little kid in me who was once reluctant to shine a little brighter. I love experimenting with all different colors: pinks, purples, reds, blues, magentas, yellows, light pinks (okay, maybe now I *am* just trying to meet the word count for this book). I also find it fascinating to clock the way other people respond to it. Not to use a broad brush, but when I'm on tour, I can usually tell what part of the country I'm in based on the reactions to my bright pink nails. For example, the Midwest: generally not overly thrilled about it; anyplace along the West Coast: tons of women asking me what color I use; Northeast: nobody gives a flying fuck (that's why I live there); Florida: good luck to me.

I was recently going through security at the Kansas City airport, shortly after the 2024 Super Bowl. The male TSA officer was visibly squeamish—dare I say displeased—when he noticed my hand as I passed him my ID. In an effort to alleviate his own discomfort, and likely more to poke fun, he glared at me as he handed it back and said in a cold, aggressively sour tone, "Go, Chiefs." (Translation: "Here's your ID, fag.") I lifted my hand with my nails facing him, spread out my fingers, and said, "Sir, does it look like I follow basketball?" Everyone around us laughed, and even he was tickled enough to let his stern expression melt into a big, goofy grin. I like to think little encounters like that have a ripple effect to help inspire more tolerance around the world. Or at least prevent large TSA officers from kicking my ass. It always helps to have a joke in your back pocket.

I'm overjoyed when I see how many people come to my live shows all glittered up, painted, and decked out in their campiest attire. Even some straight men who come with their wives to my meet-and-greets are giddy to show me their colorful manicures, done especially for me. I'm no influencer in this department, but if I'm able to contribute in some small way to the gender-inclusive beauty movement or inspire self-expression by simply having a little fun, it will be my honor. I would also be honored to accept fifty percent off my next purchase of Estée Lauder Double-Wear Foundation in shade Ivory Rose, #2C4. (Just sayin'.)

Sorry this chapter didn't include any useful contouring tips or game-changing makeup hacks like how to use Preparation H as under-eye concealer. I think I just wanted to take the opportunity to remind you that we're not on this planet forever. You should never resist a splash of "cuh-luh" if it brings you a little joy. Don't let anyone steal those simple little joys from you. Stealing in general is never good. Unless you're stealing nail polish from your fake girlfriend's Caboodle—then by all means, go right ahead. If you feel like wearing the lipstick or the high heels or the glitter or that hideous-ass blouse that you love even though no one thinks it flatters you, then don't even think twice. You are a woman of considerable means, and you're worth it.

(Call me, L'Oréal.)

12

Would That I Had an Ass

O would that I had an ass, most coveted of gay-boy bumps
What confidence, what swagger I'd exude
And yet, forsooth, no booty perches 'pon these bony stumps
For nothing from my backside doth protrude

I'd rest my whole identity on my robust patootie
All spectators wouldst doeth double-takes
Sharp intellect and wit would nevermore be mine own duty
Had only God endowed me wit' dem cakes

O would that I could have an ass like every TikTok model,
A sight from which Kardashians might plotz
I'd throw away each butt enhancement pill from ev'ry bottle
And cut out all the lunges, lifts, and squats

I'd take my ass most everywhere: the beach; for shopping; banking;
The laundromat; to Paris, London, Rome
And shouldst at any time it might require a little spanking
I'd buy my ass a drink and take it home

O tiny, little tuchus mine, O wherefore art thou tiny?
Why doth thee not submit to stair machines?

How joyous wouldst my wardrobe be if I could grow a heinie
And fin'ly fill a pair of Gucci jeans?

I'd sit for hours on wooden chairs with ne'er a doughnut pillow
Two big ol' built-in cushions 'neath my back
But O, alas, my derriere's as flat as Amarillo
A pale white sheet of drywall with a crack

O think of the external validation I'd receiveth
Had I a perky peach like Chalamet
And though mine own love interests would detest to see me leaveth
O how they'd love to watch me walk away

I'd bounce it, move it, shake it, pop it back, and drop it way low
I'd clap them cheeks and make that fanny talk
And shouldst from all this clapping cometh fame to rival JLo
Fear not; I'd still be "Randy from the block"

O, fie! Begone, the wretched flak and body-shaming strictures
Of every faceless troll and Grindr jerk
I'd saveth hours on Instagram spent doctoring my pictures
And use the time to learneth how to twerk

O wouldst that I had just been blessed back there, those folk, I'd show 'em;
From work retire and adjust my plans
For hence I'd ne'er compose another clever song or poem
And at long last, I'd joineth OnlyFans

13

How Do You Solve a Problem Like Valhalla?

Here's something that really irks me. You know when people who've been nominated for a major award are asked by the press how they learned the news, and they say some sanctimonious bullshit like "Oh, I didn't even remember the nominations were being announced. . . . I was totally sleeping. . . . My publicist called to tell me, and I was so surprised and confused because I'm a serious artist who's only motivated by creative fulfillment and not the superficial prestige of industry prizes"? I have always found these assholes to be completely phony and obnoxious. As it turns out, I am also now one of them (and I secretly kind of love it).

In November 2022, I was nominated for a Grammy Award in the category of Best Comedy Album. Now, let's cut the shit: While I am in fact a serious artist who is motivated by creative fulfillment, blah, blah, blah, I am also quite interested in superficial prizes. I am fairly competitive by nature and have a great affinity for external validation and sparkly trophies.

In elementary school, when my fifth grade teacher held a pie-eating contest at the end of the year and I was selected to participate after winning the lottery by pulling one of three red rubber balls from a box of otherwise yellow rubber balls, I cried for a week when I lost to Emily Giordano (who absolutely fucking cheated by using her hands, and I hope that snake is reading this now). In high school, when the time came for district and state thespian competitions, I rehearsed my songs and scenes more than anyone else in my class. Sure, I wanted to excel in my craft, but mostly I wanted to take home as many chintzy three-dollar plastic statues as would fit on my parents' mantel. Now, when I submit my work for Emmy Award consideration, I know exactly when the announcements will be made—date, time, and place. It's always marked in my calendar and, I can assure you, I am wide awake, sitting bright-eyed at my computer, and repeatedly hitting the refresh button until the results appear.

However, on the morning of November 15, 2022, when Machine Gun Kelly—of all people—stood at the podium onstage at the Grammy Museum in Los Angeles before a global live-streaming audience and said my name, I was not watching. I knew that my first solo studio album had been submitted but had given it no further thought beyond approving the record label's request to submit it when they had asked months earlier. It seemed like an absurdly long shot, so I forgot all about it. It was in no way on my radar that the nominations were being announced on this particular morning until a text came through from my publicist while I was making tea and brushing my teeth: HOLY SHIT YOU'RE A FUCKING GRAMMY NOMINEE!!! I was surprised and confused. Finally, I was one of those assholes.

I still couldn't bring myself to believe it. I ran to my phone with a mouthful of Colgate and pulled up the clip on YouTube. Sure enough, there, in all his hungover grunge-glam glory, was Machine Gun reading the list of nominees in the Best Comedy Album category: Patton Oswalt, Jim Gaffigan, Louis C.K., Dave Chappelle, and me. You know . . . all the gay icons.

It felt like a strange fever dream. Even as I remember it all now, it still kind of does. I have to say, for all the crazy excitement I felt as a first-time nominee, what immediately struck me the most was how proud I was that this little album by a flamboyant show queen (me) singing musical comedy show tunes was among the ranks of these uberstraight, mainstream standup comedy giants. The nomination alone felt like a small victory for theater nerds everywhere. Patton Oswalt and Jim Gaffigan both sent lovely messages that afternoon welcoming me to the club.

As if all this weren't thrilling enough, the Recording Academy soon reached out to ask if I would host the Grammy Premiere Ceremony. The Premiere Ceremony is where they give out the awards in all the categories you don't see on the main network telecast (including my category). I happily accepted, of course, and at the end of January, the producers asked if I would write a song parody for myself to sing as the show's opening. I reworked some lyrics to a Broadway classic, which they were very pleased with. They told me I would be accompanied by the full Grammy orchestra, led by the great Jeff Babko, whom I'd already worked with on *Better Things* and *Jimmy Kimmel Live*. This was all marvelous. We found a key for the song, I spent a few days rehearsing in my apartment, and a week later, I was on my way to LA for the big night.

I gave myself some extra rehearsal during the five-and-a-half-hour flight, just to be sure my lyrics were memorized. I also worked out a few softball political bits to keep in my back pocket. There had been specific instruction during initial discussions for me not to get political (a note I'm often given before hosting things like this), but I've had enough experience to know that when producers say that, they rarely mean it. In fact, they usually mean the exact opposite. There's always a slight wink in their eye. Why else would they ask a moderately polarizing figure known for political humor to host their event? I think they're just doing their due diligence, but at the end of the day (especially nowadays, when it's so *en vogue*), political jokes are to producers of nonpolitical functions what male interns are to closeted Republican congressmen: the more they protest, the more into it they probably are . . . (ALLEGEDLY!).

I landed and was on my way to the hotel to freshen up before going to rehearsal for the ceremony, which would take place the very next day. Imagine my surprise when, during the drive, an email popped up on my phone from one of the producers, telling me that there was a last-minute issue with clearances for the parody I'd written, and it would unfortunately have to be scrapped. Shit!

There I was, a jet-lagged, first-time Grammy host and nominee, hours away from the ceremony, without an opening number. Things were not off to a perfect start. Being a one-man band, I don't travel with a team of writers to assist in such emergencies. I don't *have* a team of writers. Luckily, the show's head writer was able to flesh out her script, incorporating a few of the jokes I'd written, and it wound up good enough. . . . not as fabulous as the musical extravaganza that had originally been planned, but hey, what are you gonna do?

The rehearsal at Microsoft Theater (now Peacock Theater) went well. I got in a little practice with the teleprompter and was given blocking on where to stand for my monologue and each of the categories I would subsequently be presenting, how to receive and open each envelope, and how to present the trophies to each winner. After rehearsal, on my walk out of the building, one of the writers handed me a study packet, including the names of all the nominees. A handful of phonetic spellings were highlighted for nominees with longer, potentially more challenging names. This was very much appreciated because, while my pronunciation skills are generally on point, it's not impossible for me to lose my head momentarily amidst the stress and panic of having to speak or read publicly. After all, the ceremony would be live-streamed to a large audience. I hit up a few of the Grammy gifting suites for some free shit I would never use, then brought the packet back to my hotel room and studied it like the Torah until I drifted off to sleep.

From the wings of the Microsoft the next afternoon, I heard a booming voice introduce me. I walked out to greet the audience, cameras swirling around me from every angle, took my mark center stage, and delivered my opening monologue. I got some decent laughs and was feeling pretty settled. So far, so good. I delivered my last line of the monologue: "Now, let's give out some Grammys!" As the crowd cheered and the orchestra swelled, one of the trophy presenters escorted me stage right to my second location to announce the first round of nominees. I've always heard security experts say, "You should never let them take you to a second location." I'm fairly certain they're referring to crime scenes and not the Grammy Awards; nevertheless, I should have heeded the warning.

The first award presentation went off without a hitch. I followed procedure exactly as instructed: I announced the category as it appeared on the teleprompter, said, "The nominees are . . . ," which triggered a video montage accompanied by a prerecorded voice-over introducing all the nominees and their respective projects, opened the envelope I'd just been handed, read the name as it appeared in the envelope, and stepped aside, allowing the winner to accept. Gorgeous!

It was time for the second award. The category was Best Score Soundtrack for Video Games and Other Interactive Media. I saw the intro pop up on the teleprompter and read it like a champ, which triggered the montage, and so on. This was going beautifully. I was a real pro. As I was still acclimating to the theater's acoustics, I couldn't hear the voice-over listing all the nominees over the roaring crowd, but I wasn't listening anyway. I was by now so pleased with myself that the pep talk going on inside my head was drowning out all external noise: *You're a natural, kid. They will definitely invite you back to host next year. These people love you! In fact, you're so terrific, I think they might tell Trevor Noah he can go home and ask you to host the main show. Tough break, Trev. I sure hope he takes it well.* The highlight reel finished, and I popped open the envelope to announce the winner. I lifted the flap, and to my horror, just waiting there to taunt me, was one of the phonetically spelled names. *Shit! Not now! Not yet! It's only my second envelope! I'm just finding my footing here! I'm not ready for this kind of pressure!*

All the studying I'd done the night before flew out of my head, and all confidence drained from my body. Luckily, I managed to work through my panic and deliver the winning composer's name: Stephanie Economou. I don't think it was perfect, but it was at least distinguishable enough to elicit a big ovation from the audience. *Phew!* I should have quit while I was ahead, but ever the overachiever, I continued on to announce the title of the video game listed below the composer's name: *Assassin's Creed Valhalla*.

"Valhalla" is properly pronounced "val-HALL-uh." That is not how I pronounced it.

This might come as a surprise to you, but action-adventure video games about historical-fictionalized Viking warriors are not really my thing. Viking culture in general is something I admittedly have absolutely no knowledge of or interest in. If you need help remembering specific details pertaining to any of Delta Burke's character arcs on *Designing Women*, please see me. If it's total recall of lyrics to every song from *The Sound of Music* you're after, I'm your gay. But when it comes to fortress-raiding, sword-wielding, Druid-battling, or violent virtual Viking role-play of any kind, I'm sadly of no use.

"Valhalla," which in Old Norse translates to "hall of the fallen," is a mythological heavenly Viking paradise where warriors killed in battle go in the afterlife. I just googled that because as I write about it now, I still really don't know what the hell Valhalla is. You probably didn't need me to explain it anyway, because, as I eventually found out, everyone in the free world knows what Valhalla is. Every member of my family knows. All my queeny-ass friends know and might even have summer shares there. Everyone on the Internet definitely knows. Even my pop-culturally-challenged mother, who claims to have no idea who Emily Blunt is (even though she has absolutely seen and enjoyed almost all of her films), knows—and has apparently always known—what Valhalla is. I, on the other hand, had (at least to my immediate recollection) never seen, heard, or attempted to speak the word until this moment.

There was no phonetic spelling provided because, again, everyone on Earth knows how to pronounce "Valhalla" except yours truly, and having had no time to recover from my mini–panic attack over the composer's phonetically spelled name milliseconds earlier, I panicked even more. In a fight-or-flight response, I briefly left my body and allowed my mouth full rein to say whatever my brain could manage to send it in that moment. Noticing the double-"l," which I guessed was a digraph indicating some sort of Spanish etymology, I announced in a strange accent of no identifiable origin: *"Assassin's Creed . . . V'lah-ha."*

I knew right away that I'd made a mistake, but it didn't appear to do any immediate damage. The cheers of the live audience were so loud, they didn't seem to hear it. I barely heard it myself. Maybe no one heard it. And who was really paying attention, anyway? I mean, with all due respect, I was just announcing a video game, not delivering the State of the Union.

After the winner's acceptance speech was over, I introduced the next presenter and ran offstage for my first break. My team was waiting there for me. When I asked if they had noticed anything weird about my last presentation, they assured me they had not, so I let it go and moved on.

The rest of the ceremony went smoothly, and there were many highlights. One I will never forget is having the privilege to stand onstage while Viola Davis won her first Grammy Award for the audiobook narration of her memoir, *Finding Me*, officially cementing her historic status as an EGOT winner. I was mere feet from her at the podium on the opposite end of the stage, mouth agape, as she gave her speech, the close of which was my next cue to speak. I told the audience I would need a moment. I later saw her having her makeup retouched backstage. She politely smiled at me, and I wanted so badly to run up to her and gush, but I was too nervous. Instead, I just threw one of those obnoxious clasped-hand silent head-bowings in her direction, blessing her with my reverence. Ugh, I'm a dork.

Toward the end of the ceremony, R & B legend Babyface took the stage to present the Best Comedy Album award. My group and I huddled around one of the monitors backstage to watch as all the nominees were listed one last time. Sure enough, there was my name. I don't think I completely believed any of this was real until that moment. And sure enough, I lost to Dave Chappelle, who won for his controversial Netflix special *The Closer*. He was not in attendance, so Mr. 'face accepted on his behalf. I went back onstage and announced to the audience that I had been robbed, encouraging them to join me in storming the US Capitol to demand a recount.

Once the Premiere Ceremony was over, it was time to do some press before finally sitting down to enjoy the main show. There I was on the red carpet, totally pulling focus from Taylor Swift, Sam Smith, Shania Twain, and Cardi B (at least I tried). Reporters were interviewing me, and photographers were taking my picture. For the first time that day, I really felt like a star. And lest you fear this sudden resurgence of self-confidence went straight to my head, leaving me way too big for my britches, never fear—it will all be gone by the end of the next paragraph.

I took my seat in the Crypto.com Arena. It was time to snap a few selfies before showtime and obnoxiously show off for social media; I had earned it. I opened Twitter and noticed a lot of action in my mentions. This was odd. Were all these people reaching out to congratulate me? Doubtful. Suddenly struck by the realization of what was going on without even having to look, my stomach dropped out of my butt. I started feverishly scrolling, and indeed, a clip of my "Valhalla" gaffe from just a few hours earlier was circulating and already had 850,000 views! The category was *Fuck my life.*

Thanks to the wonders of modern audio, the home livestreaming audience had no trouble hearing every muddled syllable of my bumble, and many of them had opinions. Here's a sampling of a few choice comments I thought you might enjoy:

Fuck this Pee-wee Herman looking piece of shit!

Who doesn't know how to pronounce Valhalla in 2023? Viking culture is everywhere.

Where did they find this DUMBFUCK?

A few of the more analytical conspiracy theorists speculated that I may have masterminded the whole thing. One wrote, *The pronunciation was so bad, I'm wondering if he did it on purpose. It's the kind of thing he'd do. He's got the face and name of a psychopathic dystopian game show presenter.*

I'd been spoofing Trump for years, and even the lambasting I'd gotten from MAGA Republicans had never risen to the level of the intense hostility I was now seeing over the title of a video game. I had inadvertently poked a bear I didn't even know existed and enraged what might actually be the most aggressive and vitriolic of all Internet troll subspecies: the gamer trolls.

I was so mortified and consumed by the hate parade happening in the palm of my hand, I really don't remember anything else about that amazing night. I don't remember who won what award. I don't remember any of the speeches. I don't remember the performances by Harry Styles (with whom I'm deeply in love) or Lizzo or Madonna. I don't remember sitting less than twenty feet from Beyoncé (thankfully, a grainy picture still lives on my phone, so I know it really happened). I do vaguely remember witnessing, firsthand, that awkward exchange between Ben Affleck and JLo that wound up going viral. Remember . . . ? When they didn't know the cameras were on them and everyone spent the next month trying to figure out what they were saying to each other? If I hadn't been so distracted, I definitely could have figured out what they were saying. In retrospect, I'm sure it was something like *Can you believe that dumbfuck didn't know how to pronounce "Valhalla"?* I don't even remember much of the after-party. I don't remember who I met or what fancy hors d'oeuvres I ate. Maybe worst of all, I don't remember feeling proud of myself that night. I was not present, and I feel bad about that.

Valhallagate continued for about a week and even made a little news. The popular video gaming site GameSpot posted the headline "Assassin's Creed Valhalla's Grammy Win Overshadowed by Presenter Hilariously Butchering the Game's Name." *Sports Illustrated* wrote, "Assassin's Creed Valhalla wins Grammy, though we can't be sure. . . ." Outlets like *The Today Show* picked up my official apology after I humorously addressed the issue on my own socials. Another headline from Deadline read, "Randy Rainbow

Apologizes for 'Valhalla' Grammy Flub." Oh, well, I guess all press is good press. And more importantly, I looked cute in the pictures.

The irony of my Valhalla scandalla (pronounced "scan-DALL-uh") was not lost on me. After all, I had cut my teeth mocking celebrities for very similar public blunders, like the time John Travolta infamously (and unforgivably) introduced Idina Menzel as "Adele Dazeem" at the 2014 Grammy Awards. One of my very first viral videos was a musical roast of that awkward tongue slip to the tune of "La Vie Bohème" from *Rent*. Even Anthony Rapp, who was starring with Idina on Broadway at the time in the musical *If/Then*, saw it and invited me to the show as his guest. Now, nearly a decade later, karma had finally come to pay me back in kind. What poetic justice for John Travolta.

The social media persecution persisted for days. Those gamer trolls really got their neckbeards in a twist over me. Thankfully, the good people at *Assassin's Creed* soon came to my rescue. Their official Twitter account posted a mock-up of the game's famous poster with the title misspelled as I had pronounced it ("VALHAHA") to their nearly five million followers and captioned it "We got your back Randy!" God bless those people. When the time comes, there will definitely be a place for them in Valhalla.

So what's the point of this story other than to gently remind you that I was nominated for a Grammy Award? For one thing, I guess it's a good excuse to make a meal out of this little banana peel I slipped on. It's also an opportunity to take stock of the experience. Listen, this was not a major event in my life. It wasn't even a major event of that event. Trust me, Bennifer had it much worse than I did the morning after. (Mom, "Bennifer" is what they call Ben Affleck and JLo.) It does, however, strike me as a teachable moment—if not for you, then for me. We're living in a time when the opinions and criticism and omnipresent babel of strangers follow us everywhere we go. It seems it will be this way for the foreseeable future, at least for those of us who insist on remaining technologically connected. I would like to commit to myself that I will at least make a concerted effort not to allow all that noise to drown out the well-earned joys of my life, as I did that night and have done on many other occasions—before and since. Maybe putting it here in writing is a way of indelibly holding myself to that promise. I guess that's partly what this chapter has been about. Above all, though, it's to remind you—and I can't stress this enough—that I was nominated for a Grammy Award.

I would also like to apologize once again to the *Assassin's Creed* franchise and thank them for their generosity. A few days after their adorable post in my honor, they sent me a big box of *Valhalla* T-shirts, *Valhalla* coffee mugs, and other *Valhalla* swag. Between you and me, it's still sitting in the box. Next time I'm presenting at an awards show, remind me to mispronounce something I'd actually like to take home . . . like "Mercedes-Benz" or "Harry Styles."

14

Notes from a Litter Box

How to introduce myself . . . ? I respond to so many different monikers: "boo-boo," "princess," "good girl," "stop that. . . ." And then, of course, there's my personal favorite: "Who's the prettiest girl in the whole wide world?" I like that one because I know the answer. It's me.

My pedigree certificate lists only my date of birth: July 29, 2020 (I normally maintain that a lady should never reveal her age, but I suppose it is public knowledge at this point) and my breed: Chinchilla Silver Persian. It also misgenders me as Male. That little discovery wouldn't be made until almost two weeks after I was brought home. Because of my petite frame and dainty features, my doctors and caretakers were unable to accurately identify my biology until a second visit to the hospital. They say human brains are larger, but sometimes I do wonder.

After my original boy name was scrapped, and following much tedious deliberation spanning several days, an official replacement was finally selected. I am formally called Tippi. I was never properly consulted on the matter, but I must say, it does suit me. . . . My bushy white tail ends with a flourish of silver gray at the tip. Also, I've always been very generous when it comes to the matter of gratuity for those who service me. Contrary to popular belief, I was not named for the actress Tippi

Hedren, though I've always admired her activism in support of animal rights.

Many of you surely know me as a renowned Instagram model. My page currently boasts 8,064 followers, which I'm told is more than any other cat account has on that platform. This quite pleases me, but I try not to let success go to my head. I'm just a no-frills New York City girl, living her life. I don't do tricks; I've had no formal training. I like to make my audience come to me, so to speak, rather than jump right into their laps. I've never been one to claw my way to fame like some other thirsty influencers who'll backflip at the drop of a catnip mouse if they know the camera's rolling. I won't mention names . . . (MrMarbles38). For the record, I have not personally seen any of the financial revenue generated from my content to date. Still, it's steady work, and I'm glad to have it.

Perhaps I'm best known, though, as the trusty and adorable companion of Randy Rainbow, who, by his own account, is, as well, a prominent public figure and celebrated icon of the stage and screen. (He does mention this quite often, though I've yet to verify.) I, however, know him for what he truly is: my faithful courtier and personal chef. I don't mean to oversimplify our relationship, mind you. He is many things to me: mother, father, kitten. . . . The dynamic between us is one of great complexity.

Truth be told, I had certain reservations about him at the time of my adoption. I thought surely it was just a publicity stunt, a cheap attention-grab. After all, you know homosexuals of a certain maturity with no human children of their own. They seem to feel inadequate in public parks and outdoor brunch settings without a gaudy designer pet carrier in tow. I really had no interest in being anyone's accessory. I suppose that's why I spent my first few days and nights under a nightstand, playing hard-to-get. I eventually came out once I realized his intentions were pure, and I have enjoyed my time here ever since. That said, I do have a few notes.

Punctuality is of the utmost importance. My schedule is so full, flexibility of time is not a luxury I can afford, nor do I tolerate it in anyone attending to me. Unfortunately, this often seems to be a great challenge for him. I like to get an early start. I wake up every morning at 6:45 a.m. sharp. I then begin my morning ablutions, applying the old-fashioned method: licking myself (I don't believe in soap or water faucets). I begin with my tushy region and, once I've determined that's pristine, move directly to phase two: his face. Though he is often resistant to this routine (at least the chronology), I know what's best for my giant furless kitten. I have, after all, retained many of my maternal instincts, regardless of the procedure I received early on without my consent, rendering me unable to conceive. A feline's right to choose has sadly been under attack for longer than I've been alive, but I shouldn't get political here. Thankfully, other than removing my ovaries and my uterus, he's been very respectful of my bodily autonomy. Except for the one time he tried to put me in a Halloween costume. That didn't end well.

I've usually worked up quite an appetite by the time we've both had our baths. Then it's time to pounce on his chest and berate him until he gets up to feed me. I do my best vocalizing first thing in the morning—I find it's a nice way to warm up my cords in preparation for the rest of the day. Though I'm screaming loudly and unpleasantly into his ear, he sometimes manages to drift back off to sleep, which is when I begin gently tapping the bridge of his nose with my paw in a consistent rhythm until he's regained consciousness. If this does not work, I apply additional force, smacking him violently on the head. By now I'm famished and have no intention of being ignored.

Finally, he is up and stumbling toward the place he calls Kitchen, a special room built exclusively to store my vast array of food and treat products. I'm really hollering at him now. I'm so hungry that I can barely contain the raw emotion boiling over in me. By the sounds of my anguished yowls, you would think I hadn't eaten in months or that I was being assaulted. I can tell he's getting nervous. Surely he'll be reported to the ASPCA for abuse and neglect if any of the neighbors hear my screams. He desperately pries open the can, one eye still half shut, and pours the contents into my bowl. I'm now tearing at the leg of his pajamas, pleading—begging him to put me out of my misery, to stop the unbearable pangs of hunger that will surely kill me if I'm left to endure them a moment longer. Finally, he places the bowl down on the floor before me. I rush to it, take precisely one lick, then shake my paw at the bowl and walk away, signaling I've had enough. Breakfast is now over, and I am tranquil once again.

It's very important to remain properly hydrated. I like to follow each meal with a trip to my water bowl, which I insist be freshened regularly throughout the day. Temperature is key. My drinking water—always filtered, never tap—should always be approximately 62 degrees Fahrenheit. If it rises above 65 degrees, I'd sooner not go anywhere near it. I don't want anyone to lose his job over this, but on more than one occasion over the years, it has been room temperature.

After breakfast, I take to my favorite chair under the desk in a place he calls the Live-in Groom. I have a very fine view from my chair. I can see the entire whole wide world, which, you should know, runs from one end of the street in front of our apartment house all the way to the other. I sit and stare until I can see the orange-and-yellow fire come up over the brown boxes that sit in the green before me. Such pretty colors. If I look up, I can usually see the roof of the big blue cat tent above, with the fluffy white balls that dangle from it and the birds that often disappear into them. Sometimes the birds swoop down close enough to the window for me to try to catch them, but I fear I may never be victorious. When I look down, I can see all the little cat toys zooming every which way along the street spanning the whole wide world. He sits beside me in his favorite chair with his cup of morning tea, and I'm always happy to share the view with him. It is quite a sight, and I think I am quite a lucky cat.

By 7:50 a.m., I turn to find his favorite chair empty and fear the worst. I leap off my chair and run down the hall to look for him. Sure enough, my worst fears are indeed well-founded. He is once again rummaging through my litter box. This happens every single morning. The shock and humiliation rock me to my core each time. I force myself to watch in horror as he proceeds to violate my most sacred and intimate property, patronizing me all the while with inappropriate comments about my pee-pees and doodies. Once he finally vacates the premises with my very personal belongings, I quickly jump into the box and immediately replace everything he has unlawfully stolen.

There are two things about which I am most passionate: cookies and playing. I may be a career woman, but I still find time to enjoy all the recreational pleasures of life. After I've had my first five morning treats (and yes, the portions must be no more or fewer than five), it's time for him to break from his daily chores and play a fun game with me. I aggressively insist, in my highest soprano, that he make it his urgent business to do so.

Two of my favorite games include "Chase the Shoelace" and "I See You!" (more colloquially known as "hide-and-seek"). He is often quite good at these games, but there are times, I regret to report, when he "phones in" his performance. This very much displeases me, and I will usually pause the game to make it known. *Where is the feeling behind anything you're doing?* my eyes communicate through a withering glare. I always try to encourage a Stanislavskiesque approach. I want him to *become* the wildebeest in the woodlands of the Serengeti, trying to escape my fierce hunting prowess. I want him to really *inhabit* the shoelace. Sometimes his heart just isn't in it.

I suppose the insatiable distraction of his precious phone toy does not help matters. My, but they do love those things, don't they? If during the course of our game—or really at any time—his focus is diverted for too long, I will resort to biting his ankles. Not forcefully enough to draw blood, mind you; just a few pecks to remind him where his concentration must always be unwaveringly fixed (on me).

I take many naps before dinnertime. Posing for as many photographs as I do in a day can be taxing. I'm again quite starved, both for snacks and attention, when I awaken from a nap. I expect always to be greeted with a tasty treat and/or light chin rubs. As I have tried to teach him, each emergence from my slumber should be considered a call to action. I cannot stress enough that chin rubs, or any type of physical affection, for that matter, must always be initiated by yours truly. Excessive petting is an infringement usually perpetrated by emotionally stunted humans with no boundaries. No cat enjoys this, especially when it is unauthorized. Still, it happens far too frequently, which is what led me to launch the #MeowToo movement on social media.

After dinner, another few hundred rounds of "Chase the Shoelace," and some late-night moving-picture-watching, it's time to prepare for our longest, deepest catnap of the evening. I really like that one. I give myself another quick bath and begin drifting off to the shapes and flickering lights of his favorite programs. I sprawl out across our blanket, generously leaving him roughly twenty-three percent of the mattress space. I always sleep through the night. It's important that I get adequate beauty rest for the new day ahead.

While I find my preferred self-bathing techniques more than efficient, he sometimes feels that outside assistance is necessary. On these days, he puts me in my gaudy pink cat purse, which I really love, and takes me to Groomer . . . which I really do not. Groomer does not respect my water faucet–free preferences and, even more offensively, always uses "he/him" pronouns when addressing me. Considering how handsy Groomer is, you'd think Groomer would be familiar enough with my anatomy by now to get it right. I do not like these days. However, knowing how important it is for a woman to always be coiffed, fragrant, and ready to impress her favorite beau, I grin and bear it. Of course, a hundred milligrams of Gabapentin doesn't hurt. I do also love my pills.

Now, don't be alarmed, but when we're at home, he sometimes raises his voice to me. It's infrequent but not beyond the realm of possibility. Usually it is when I try to go behind the hot drying machine while it's running or leap from the tall counter in Kitchen or try to sniff the bottles that hold chemicals for cleaning. He seems to detect danger in these actions. What he fails to realize is that I have no suicidal ideation; constantly finding new ways to potentially kill myself is merely a relaxing hobby. He especially dislikes when I play with the paper hanging from the roll mounted on the wall beside the toilet. I think this is quite rich, considering the unspeakable things *he* does with that paper.

Our Friday and Saturday nights can get rowdy. Occasionally, we have visitors. I like visitors. I delight them by lying on my back and showing them my belly. A hostess must always go above and beyond to entertain her guests. Sometimes, when we're alone, he'll put on music and have what he calls "dance parties." He jumps around the Live-in Groom ferociously, sipping a cocktail, while I observe. He'll often change the lyrics to certain songs, personalizing them just for me. Some of my past favorites have included "Oh Tippi, you're so fine . . ." and "Tippi Rainbow is the girl I love . . ." to the tune of "Bloody Mary" from *South Pacific*. In all honesty, the whole display—while amusing—can be rather cringeworthy. But it seems to make him happy, and I like that very much.

He isn't always happy, though. There are days when he is quite sad. He stays in bed longer than usual on those days, and it can be an arduous task motivating him to play our daily games. I try to be compassionate. I don't take his lack of enthusiasm personally. I know he still loves me. It's just human nature, I guess. I really don't like those days. I'm very sensitive to the things he feels, you see, and that can weigh heavily on a companion. But he's always there for me when I'm not feeling my best, so I'm always there for him.

Even worse are the days when he leaves. I know those days are coming because I begin to hear the dreaded zipping sounds of many zippers (never a good sign). I know he will soon go on the other side of what he calls the Frundoore and I won't see him for a long time. Sometimes he stays on the other side for days. I know there are many long-standing conspiracy theories promoting the idea that we have no concept of time, but I can assure you that's inaccurate. I spend most of those days on the rug by the Frundoore, neglecting my favorite activities and napping spots. He always leaves the moving pictures on for me, which I appreciate (preferred channels: CNN, Disney Junior, and the birds and butterflies channel). And I'm attended to by many nursemaids (one of whom he recently dismissed after learning that she was getting into the medicine cabinet). They're all nice enough. They feed me and make sure I get my treats and my play time. It isn't the same, though.

Worst of all is that he never says goodbye when he leaves. I know it's because he read somewhere that making a big fuss will only upset me and that it's better to just slip out quietly. I don't know where he read that. Probably in the same stupid article that said cats have no concept of time. I know he means well, and I know he will always come back eventually. Still . . . I wish he'd say goodbye.

I don't know what I'm doing in this whole wide world. I really don't know what it's all about. Sometimes I can tell he feels the same. Much of it is confusing and often makes me scared. A lot of it (particularly Groomer) just irritates me. For the most part, though, I'd say I'm quite content. Somehow I know I'm where I belong . . . with my giant furless kitten beside me. I don't know how long we will be here together. I hope for a long time. I don't know where I'll go next. But if the day comes that I must leave him, as I have heard is often the natural order, I know I will continue to watch over him, perhaps from behind the white fluffy balls that dangle from the big blue cat tent above our apartment house, where those darn birds always disappear. Perhaps there will be a new companion beside him then, sitting in my favorite chair and looking out at all the pretty colors below me. Yes, I'll always watch over him and care for him just as he has always done for me (though imperfectly at times), because he is mine and I am his. I think it really is a very nice whole wide world, and I'm happy to be the prettiest girl in it.

15

Ladies and Gentlemen . . .
My Mother (the Sequel)

We're live in three, two . . .

And welcome back, folks! We're joined now by a very special guest for what is being called by many in the industry "the most highly anticipated sequel since *Top Gun: Maverick*." You know her, you love her, you want some more of her! Please put your hands together for my mom, Gwen, because who knows better than the Jewish mother of a gay man how to solve America's problems?

(APPLAUSE)

Randy: *Hello, Mother darling.*

Mom: *Hello, my child.*

Randy: *Well, our chapter in my last book was such a huge hit, my editor insisted you make a comeback. How does it feel to be so in demand?*

Mom: *It's not a comeback; it's a return.*

Randy: *Okay, Norma Desmond. It's amazing we could even get you, what with your full schedule. Not to mention your appearance fees. For a while, there was talk of replacing you with Dianne Wiest.*

Mom: *Dianne Wiest isn't a bad second choice. I wouldn't be offended.*

Randy: *Speaking of my first memoir, your college-dropout son is officially a* New York Times *best-selling author. Can you even?*

Mom: *I think this is your most unexpected accomplishment.*

Randy: *Thank you. Please do continue with your backhanded compliment.*

Mom: *No, it really is. Never did I think you would be an author at all, let alone a best-selling author. You barely read!*

Randy: *Please wrap it up.*

Mom: *I'm very proud of you. And thanks for keeping me stocked with copies of the first book.*

Randy: *You mean* Playing with Myself, *now available in paperback wherever books are sold?*

Mom: *Yes, that one. I keep them in the trunk of my car for emergencies. Someone asked me to autograph a copy. I had no idea what to write, so I wrote about three paragraphs of "Thanks, and have a great life, and follow your dreams, and you should live and be well" . . . and then you told me you just sign your name. I wish I had known that.*

Randy: *You haven't been a major celebrity for very long. You'll learn.*

Mom: *I am much more famous now, though. I no longer give my name as "Gwen" when someone asks. I now go by "Gwen Rainbow do you know my son Randy Rainbow?"*

Randy: *Terrific. Maybe stop doing that.*

Mom: *And if they say they do not, I tell them I'm embarrassed for them.*

Randy: *Good, that's just the kind of publicity I want. Anyway, what does this kind of cachet buy you at your monthly seniors book club? Are there any new perks involved? Free food? A tiara? The perfervid adulation of your peers?*

Mom: *"Perfervid adulation"?*

Randy: *I'm a fancy author now. I say shit like that.*

Mom: *Calm down, Herman Melville. Wait, what did you just ask me?*

Randy: *Perks . . .*

Mom: *Oh, yeah. So far, no perks from my book club. You'd think I'd at least get a free appetizer or something. I'll mention it to the ladies at the next meeting.*

Randy: *That's bullshit. My book was even an official selection of your monthly book club, right?*

Mom: *That's right. They insisted!*

Randy: *So, give it to me straight. How were the reviews?*

Mom: *Everyone gave the book a 10. I have no idea if anyone read it.*

Randy: *I'll accept that. As long as you read it.*

Mom: *I not only read it, I listened to the audiobook. Wait, I was on the audiobook! That was a hoot. They drove me to a recording studio and put me in a booth, and you read your part from New York, and I read mine from Fort Lauderdale.*

Randy: *Yes, I know. I was there.*

Mom: *It was really fun to do that. I just wish I sounded more like Dianne Wiest.*

Randy: *No arguments here.*

Mom: *I would also like the record to show that I have not received one thin dime in royalties.*

Randy: *Check's in the mail. I did air some of our dirty laundry in that first book. You and I talked about most of it during my writing process, but how did you experience it after the book came out?*

Mom: *Reading my dirty-laundry stories is quite different from living them. And realizing that people I would never know were now privy to so much of my private life was interesting. I would* meet people at your shows, and they would recite back to me portions of my life. I never knew exactly how to respond to that. It's a little unnerving.

Randy: *You should be very happy with my portrayal of you. You read Barbra Streisand's memoir. Compared to the things she said about her mother, I'd say you came out smelling like a rose.*

Mom: *Oy, I think I smell like the entire New York Botanical Gardens compared to her mother.*

Randy: *Let's not go overboard. Actually, that reminds me . . . one story I did not divulge was the time you tried to lose me in Disney World when I was eight, which I would say is the root of most of my adult abandonment issues. Would you care to tell the nation exactly what happened there?*

Mom: *What are you talking about?*

Randy: *Oh, please, don't try and pretend you don't remember.*

Mom: *Randy, I have no idea what you're talking about. The only thing we ever lost at Disney World was that little red autograph book that you had signed by all your favorite characters. We were bereft trying to retrace our steps and find it that whole day. Finally, we gave up and went for dinner at the Grand Floridian, and when we got back, there was the book on your bed in the hotel room, signed by Mickey and Snow White and all the other characters! It was so sweet of them to do that.*

Randy: *Are you fucking kidding me right now? You don't remember the time at EPCOT when I was eight, and we were at the IllumiNations light show at night, and I asked you for money* to go buy one of those spinny light toy things, and when I came back, you were nowhere to be found?

Mom: *Oh, God, I completely forgot about that.*

Randy: *I find it curious that you remember every detail about losing a two-dollar autograph book but have no recollection of losing your own child.*

Mom: *Stop it. You make it sound like we tried to lose you.*

Randy: *If it looks like Donald Duck and quacks like Donald Duck . . .*

Mom: *You got lost! You went back to the wrong spot. You eventually found us. Listen, it's not my fault you have no sense of direction.*

Randy: *This kind of victim blaming is unacceptable.*

Mom: *Can we move on, please?*

Randy: *Well, I wasn't planning to bring this up, but I did reveal earlier in this book that I used to sneak into your closet before you came home from work and try on your high heels. I was thirty. Just kidding. How do you respond?*

Mom: *You really did that? That's funny. Well, I guess I had it coming after all those arts-and-craft projects with the sequins and the feathers we did when you were a kid.*

Randy: *Yes, crafting is definitely at the root of all this.*

Mom: *I just can't believe I used to wear high heels.*

Randy: *I knew you would say that. On this subject, there are moms of young gay kids in my audience who would like your advice on how to do it right.*

Mom: *I do get asked this at your shows. I just let you be you. And I celebrated you for who you are. I would also tell them to put a lock on their closets if they have nice shoes.*

Randy: *It's not a bad idea. You're very active on social media these days, and your numbers are really growing. . . .*

Mom: *Yeah, I think I'm more popular on social media than you now.*

Randy: *You know who has a really strong social media presence?*

Mom: *Who?*

Randy: *Gypsy Rose Blanchard. Maybe I should take a few tips from her.*

Mom: *Watch it, smart-ass.*

Randy: *Don't worry, I'm more of a Gypsy Rose Lee type. You're really only into Instagram, though, right? Why is that?*

Mom: *I do love my Instagram! It has the best cat videos. I have no patience with the other sites. Forget X. I didn't even use it when it was Twitter. All the politics! Feh! TikTok I have no idea how to use. I can just about manage Facebook, and I enjoy look-ing at pictures of people I went to high school with who look worse than me. It's a real pick-me-up.*

Randy: *A lot has happened over the last couple of years. Let's catch everybody up. You're newly retired, or at least well on your way. How are you feeling about that?*

Mom: *Retirement is like your very first day of school. You don't want to get out of bed, you don't want to get dressed, you don't want to get on the bus, but you do, and then you can't remember when you did anything else. I am somewhat new to it, but I think I'm going to really like it.*

Randy: *What are your big plans for this exciting next chapter of your life?*

Mom: *Well, I'm volunteering at the library, taking some exercise classes, seeing my friends during the week, which is unheard-of when you're working, and of course my favorite pastime: going to doctors. Since I've retired, my calendar is filled every day with another doctor appointment. I don't know how I managed to stay alive all these years without all these doctors.*

Randy: *You're still living in South Florida with Ron DeSantis. It's so MAGA of you. I know your relationship with Florida is complicated.*

Mom: *No kidding. The weather is beautiful, but DeSantis is a nightmare. Thank God his presidential campaign crashed and burned.*

Randy: *Tell us how you really feel.*

Mom: *He has made living here hell politically and morally, not to mention dangerous if you're anything other than White,* *straight, and moronic. And forget trying to stay healthy here now. No one gets vaccinated for anything! Right now, we have a measles outbreak in my county with a side of cholera!*

Randy: *Have you supported any local drag brunches lately?*

Mom: *No, but I would love to. You know I love drag queens. Can you hold on a second? I have to use the ladies' room.*

Randy: *Yes, go ahead. . . .*

Mom: *Okay, I'm back. God, I'm drinking so much water, I can't stop peeing. It's amazing . . . one minute I don't have to pee, and then all of a sudden, I have to pee.*

Randy: *That's a great story, Ma. I think we're definitely on our way to another bestseller.*

Mom: *What else would you like to know?*

Randy: *It's been a whole book since we last checked in on your romantic life, and you're still single. How's all that going? Have you been putting yourself out there? Any new dating apps?*

Mom: *My romantic life . . . please. I am not in the least bit interested in online dating. I know it works for other people, but not me. I am very happy to have friends and family and a cat. I do worry about falling, but that's why we have Apple watches. Because if you fall, it will call 911. Why date when you can just buy a watch?*

Randy: *You've always been a hopeless romantic. Now I know where I get it.*

Mom: *You're single because you don't date anyone. If you joined an organization with other single guys, you would meet someone in five minutes!*

Randy: *You mean like the Proud Boys?*

Mom: *I'm being serious. Anyway, it's not your fault. You're never home long enough to do anything but change the litter box and wash your underwear.*

Randy: *Thank you. I'm sure once all the single hotties reading this learn how sexy my life is, they'll come flocking.*

Mom: *I have a feeling you'll meet a nice guy next year. Maybe the year after that. Whoever he is, just make sure he's kind and ethical and generous.*

Randy: *I'm really only interested in looks and money.*

Mom: *That's fine, too.*

Randy: *Speaking of litter boxes, I'm sure all the cat people and lesbians in my audience, of which there are many, will be thrilled to know you adopted a new cat.*

Mom: *Yes! Last year, I adopted a seven-year-old male domestic long-haired cat named Jack from a local shelter. But on our first vet visit, I was told that Jack was in fact Jill—a female, which many of your followers will remember is exactly the same thing that happened to you when you got your Tippi—originally Sweeney Todd.*

Randy: *I love that both of our cats are so gender fluid. It's très chic.*

Mom: *Well, I love her. I renamed her Ruby, for your birthstone. Then I thought of* The Wizard of Oz *and figured I should add Slippers. So, officially, I renamed her Ruby Slippers Rainbow.*

Randy: *That is the gayest thing you've ever done.*

Mom: *Giving birth to you is the gayest thing I've ever done.*

Randy: *Touché. Speaking of birth, my friends and cousins are all popping out kids lately. Yet here I am, still completely barren and self-involved. Have you made peace with the fact that I might not ever give you human grandchildren?*

Mom: *It gives me great joy to not have to think about grandchildren. I thoroughly enjoy my great-nieces and great-nephews, and thanks to your half-sister, Cindy, stepgrandchildren. There is no one right way to live a life. We do what feels right for us. It's the only way to live satisfied. I am quite certain that if I felt differently, I would have had more kids back when I had you.*

Randy: *And most of them would surely still be lost at EPCOT.*

Mom: *Oh, get over it. We found you eventually.*

Randy: *I believe the last time we did this, you threatened my life if I didn't introduce you to Alan Cumming. You have not yet technically been introduced, but thanks to me, you have since received a personal video message from him.*

Mom: *I still have to meet him, already! The video message he did is one of my prized possessions, but I'm still not satisfied.*

Randy: *Well, you're in luck. A running theme of this book is complaining. Other than not enough Alan Cumming in your life, what's annoying you most these days?*

Mom: *How much time do you have? You know what really annoys me? Loud people. Use your inside voice, everybody. Especially outside.*

Randy: *You've got a nerve making noise complaints. Every time I call you, I end up complaining to you about the incessant noise coming from your end of the phone. What the hell is going on over there? It sounds like you're a short-order cook in a busy Manhattan diner.*

Mom: *You have the hearing sensitivity of a bat. I'm not responsible for your inability to deal with the slightest bit of noise.*

Randy: *"Slightest bit"? It sounds like you're on a construction site in Yemen.*

Mom: *So stop calling me when I'm making dinner!*

Randy: *It sounds like you're doing foley work for a* John Wick *film.*

Mom: *No, I'm not doing that.*

Randy: *You're a retired South Floridian cat lady. The loudest noise I should hear coming from you is the occasional scrape of a shuffleboard stick and maybe* Wheel of Fortune *playing in the background.*

Mom: *I'm retired; I'm not dead.*

Randy: *Why do you think everything annoys us all the time? Are we hypoglycemic or just Jewish?*

Mom: *To be annoyed is to be aware of what the world should be and then be faced with what it is. It's amazing to me that more people aren't annoyed all the time.*

Randy: *I'll drink to that. One trait I definitely inherited from you is always being right about everything. When did you first know you had the gift?*

Mom: *I inherited that gift from my mother. She was absolutely right about all things.*

Randy: *You have strong opinions about many things, even the promotion of this book. What were some of the ideas you wanted me to relay to my publisher?*

Mom: *Well, one chapter in particular I thought would make a great guest essay in the* New Yorker. *And you should definitely be booked on all major late-night and daytime talk shows as well as* 60 Minutes, CBS Sunday Morning, *and* CNN News Central. *It would also be good if you could get David Sedaris to write the intro. And maybe a photo shoot with Alan Cumming and me holding copies of the book while taking a carriage ride in Central Park. See what you can do.*

Randy: *Who needs a publicist? Meanwhile, I have a few ideas of my own. In fact, I just announced a few chapters ago that I'm running for president.*

Mom: *Oh, is that so?*

Randy: *Yeah, I never got a callback for that untitled Ryan Murphy thing, so I figure I need to line some things up. Can I count on your endorsement?*

Mom: *I'll definitely consider you.*

Randy: *They say, "The hand that rocks the cradle . . . ," and believe it or not, I actually do take your advice from time to time. What are some issues you would like me to resolve once I'm sworn into office?*

Mom: *Health care affordability! This is very serious. We have some of the best health care systems and brightest doctors and professionals in the world and the absolute worst record for getting people affordable health care. We need low-cost health care for all in this country. Why don't you run on that?*

Randy: *I'm taking notes.*

Mom: *Also women's rights and equality. I can't understand what's going on in this country. Our laws should not be based in the beliefs of any one religion. Some of the Supremes are having a hard time understanding separation of church and state with their laws.*

Randy: *I don't know what Diana Ross has to do with this, but I hear you. This is all good stuff. Anything else?*

Mom: *Yes. Please ban the following: scented fabric softener, smoking, loud music, speeding, and retractable dog leashes.*

Randy: *Now this is getting a little too controversial. You could* *be considered for my VP if Ryan Gosling isn't available. Are you prepared to serve if called upon?*

Mom: *I'm ready, willing, and able.*

Randy: *You are on the board of your homeowners' association, or whatever. What leadership skills have you acquired in your position that would make you a qualified candidate?*

Mom: *Excuse me, I am the secretary of our board of directors for our homeowners' association. Please get that right. It's a very important position. I'm also in charge of sending violation notices to homeowners who do not follow the condo rules, and yes, I'm prepared to take my expertise to a national level.*

Randy: *Where were you on the afternoon of January 6, 2021? Just checking.*

Mom: *Don't worry; I was home, cursing at my TV.*

Randy: *You're not expecting to move into the White House with me, are you?*

Mom: *You don't even let me stay with you in your apartment when I come to New York. So no. Put me in a hotel.*

Randy: *Good. Who do I look like? Mamie Eisenhower?*

Mom: *Maybe a little around the eyes. You know, George Washington bought his mother a home after he became president.*

Randy: *I just bought you a brand-new iPhone case. Don't push* it. *Speaking of presidential parents, Lillian Carter published two of her own books during her son's presidency. My election could land you a book deal of your very own. Will you take an oath that it won't be a tell-all about me?*

Mom: *I don't know about that. You'll have to talk to my lawyer.*

Randy: *I'm also gonna need you to solemnly swear that you will not read Chapter 4 of this book.*

Mom: *Why not?*

Randy: *Just trust me on this one.*

Mom: *Whatever.*

Randy: *You could be like Rose Kennedy.*

Mom: *Yeah, she was the matriarch of an entire political dynasty. That sounds like me.*

Randy: *You're the matriarch of one single bitchy queen who does political commentary.*

Mom: *Same difference.*

Randy: *She had a cocktail named after her. What would your cocktail consist of?*

Mom: *Let's see . . . my cocktail would be 1 bottle of chocolate Glucerna protein drink mixed with ¼ cup peanut butter, a frozen banana, and 3 ice cubes. Blend until smooth. The Gwendeeni Martini!*

Randy: *Now I need a drink. Thankfully, they're giving us the high sign. But before we wrap up, I suppose it's only fair to give you the last word. I gave you shit about your rackety phone conduct, so now the floor is yours. Go on and tell America your biggest complaint about me—your beloved, firstborn and only child, whom you once tried to abandon at Disney World.*

Mom: *Thank you for finally asking. America, my biggest complaint about my son, Randy Rainbow, is—*

Randy: *So sorry, Mom, it looks like we're all out of time. Let's hear it for my mom, ladies and gentlemen!*

(APPLAUSE)

Mom: *Thank you for having me. This is now becoming a tradition.*

Randy: *Yes, we'll do it again soon.*

Mom: *Next year in EPCOT.*

Randy: *I'll bring the breadcrumbs.*

16

Memos to My Upstairs Neighbor: An Emotional Odyssey in Six Parts

Part One: The Affable Approach

Hello from your downstairs neighbor!

I'm writing to ask for your cooperation regarding a noise problem I've recently encountered. Several times over the past few months—specifically between the hours of 2 a.m. and 5 a.m.—I have been awakened by the sound of heavy walking and, less frequently, what sounds like objects being dropped/rolled on the floor of your apartment, as well as loud talking and other various sounds. I'm sure it is not your intention to be disruptive, but due to the confined living quarters and low ceilings in our building, every sound is amplified to the tenant below. Welcome to New York, right? Unfortunately, your main living area seems to be directly above my main sleeping area. I understand that we all keep different schedules, but I do wonder if you would kindly be more conscious of your volume level and perhaps walk a bit softer during late and overnight hours. You're otherwise a very considerate neighbor, and I so appreciate that. If you'd like to discuss further, you know where to find me!

Thanks in advance!
Randy
Apt. 3E

Part Two: The Gentle Reminder

Hi again!

I hope this finds you well. Just following up on my last note. It wasn't taped to your front door when I checked this morning, so I'm pretty sure you received it. By the way, I was careful to use removable Scotch tape so as not to damage your paint job. I recently got a four-pack of it on Amazon for a great price. They're having a sale. I'd be happy to share the link with you if it's of interest. Just let me know! I think it's called Magic Tape. The reason I'm writing again is because the noise issue I mentioned unfortunately seems to be ongoing. I was once again awakened by loud thumping and banging noises, as well as loud talking. I also heard music this time. I happen to be a big Phil Collins fan myself, so no complaints in that department, lol! I just wonder if you wouldn't mind keeping it down during late and overnight hours.

Thank you again for
considering my request.
Randy
Apt. 3E

Part Three: The Passive-Aggressive Bribe

Hi.

Everything okay up there? I haven't gotten a response to my initial correspondence and continue to hear those noises. The music is still too loud, and last night there was more loud banging. I'm not sure what that sound is, but it's kind of like ba-BANG . . . ba-

BANG . . . ba-BANG . . . ba-BANG. . . . It's possible you might just walk with a heavy gait, but I'm concerned that you are falling down repeatedly or perhaps trying to escape. Do you need help? You're certainly not obligated to disclose any medical conditions that might be causing you to make those highly abnormal sounds. I just want to make sure you're not being held captive and forced to listen to soft-rock hits of the '80s against your will at three o'clock in the morning, lol. (The "lol" was for my Phil Collins reference; I don't find anything funny about domestic violence.) Again, any effort to keep the noise to a minimum, especially overnight, would be greatly appreciated.

> Thanks, and please enjoy
> the bottle of wine I'm
> leaving with this note.
> Randy
> Apt. 3E

Part Four: The Desperate Plea

I don't know why you're doing this to me. I know you're getting these, because I see you took the bottle of wine. I mean, you obviously don't feel I deserve my basic right to peace and quiet—I don't know why I'm surprised that you wouldn't grant me the respect of a simple response. Yet here we are! I know you had guests last night, too. I heard every word of your conversation. Please tell your friend Lorraine I hope she patches things up with her mother. Listen, I don't want to be this person. I'm not usually this person. I mean, yes, I'm controlling. I know that about myself, and I'm trying to work on that. It's just that I haven't slept in weeks. The noise from your apartment is incessant, and I don't know what to do anymore. My work is slipping, and my personal

relationships are suffering. And it's not just that I'm controlling . . .
I have been diagnosed with a disorder that makes me extremely
sensitive to all sound. It's a real thing. It was a self-diagnosis
through an online quiz, but the results were very conclusive. And
that's not meant to invalidate my experience here. I mean, I think
we both know that your living habits are wildly erratic and you
need to accept accountability in all this. We have to make this
work somehow, and I'm just hoping that you will meet me halfway.
Please. Just . . . please.

Thank you in advance.

Me

Part Five: The Final Reckoning

It's pretty clear what's going on here. You're just messing with
me now. I know you can hear me banging on my ceiling in the
middle of the night, and yet you just keep blasting your music
and walking around in what I can only assume are the world's
heaviest steel-toed work boots. Why are you walking so much?
Where are you going? And what the hell is with all the dropping
and rolling sounds? Does your clothing keep catching fire, or did
you somehow manage to install a bowling alley in your piece-of-
shit su-su-studio apartment with all of twelve square feet? It must
be nice to be the only person occupying this building—and the
universe! I wish I could walk around (ALL DAMN NIGHT) with that
level of arrogant disregard for others—seems like fun!!! I know the
city council rep for this district. He goes to my gym, if you know
what I mean. I'll be calling him this afternoon, and he will not be
happy to hear this.

TURN DOWN YOUR MUSIC!!!

R

Part Six: Acceptance

Well, I guess we both knew this day would eventually come. I'm moving out. I found a place uptown. The location really isn't ideal for me, but the price is decent and the walls aren't so paper-thin that I can literally hear the sounds of my next-door neighbors digesting their food, like I can in this stupid building. So it's all yours. Happy now??? You win! This will be my final note. Please do not respond to it, not that you ever have before. I hope you have a great life and finally find whatever the hell it is you're so desperately searching for when roaming around your apartment like a lunatic at all hours.

PS: I never used removable Scotch tape on any of these notes. It was the regular kind, and I hope it chipped your paint. Fuck you, and fuck Phil Collins.

Randy
Apt. 3BYEEEEEE!!!

17

Declaration of Cancellation

It has come to my attention that I am not perfect. (I know . . . I couldn't believe it, either.) In fact, like many of you, I am rather flawed, and my past is indeed complicated. I have always tried my best to be a responsible, kind, and law-abiding citizen. My intentions have always been pure, but in my thirty-two years on this planet, I have, on several occasions, fallen short of God's glory and committed unforgivable sins, not the least of which is constantly lying about my age.

Cancel culture is brutal these days. I know all my closeted skeletons will inevitably be dug up and paraded through the streets when the day comes that I am finally elected to political office or, more importantly, cast as ABC's newest Gay Bachelor. This will undoubtedly lead to speculation, innuendo, fake news, and eventual prosecution by the highest court in our land . . . The Court of Public Opinion.

Therefore, **I, Randy Rainbow of the United States** of America, in order to get ahead of any possible future mass public shaming, castigation, or ostracism; ensure social and professional tranquility (for myself); provide for the common defense (of myself); promote my general welfare; and secure the blessings of the social media mob, do hereby cancel myself, effective immediately.

There . . . all done! I'm so relieved that's outta the way.

In the interest of full transparency, here is the complete list of all my worst offenses to date. "How incredibly brave of you, Randy," you say? Yes, I suppose so, but I'd rather you hear it from me. To signify the grave importance of this declaration and the sincerity of my repentance for these transgressions, I will use fancy Roman numerals. (No need to further investigate, Maggie Haberman. I have nothing to hide.)

Article I. I have never seen an entire episode of *Glee*.

Article II. I did not vote in the *American Idol* election of 2007. In my defense, I had just been broken up with by a boy whom I really liked, and there was a lot going on for me emotionally that week. Let the record show that my candidate, Jordin Sparks, handily won that year, and I have since publicly apologized to her (just now, in this book).

Article III. In 2002, shortly after moving to New York City, I shoplifted a bottle of Olay Complete moisturizer from a Duane Reade drugstore in midtown on Eighth Avenue. In my defense, I was young and poor and only trying to provide for my young pores. I was consumed by my fear of fine lines, but that does not excuse my actions. I have since made a substantial donation to the Duane Reade Charitable Foundation, which (before the chain was acquired by the Walgreens Company) supported programs designed to promote health and wellness and address vital community needs in the New York Metro area.

Article IV. I made no such substantial donation to the Duane Reade Charitable Foundation.

Article V. I accepted a complimentary ticket to a preview performance of the Broadway musical version of *Dr. Zhivago* in 2015 and left at intermission. I later told the friend who offered me the ticket that he "really shined in the second act."

Article VI. I hoarded a large quantity of pocket-sized Bath & Body Works scented hand sanitizers during COVID. I didn't actively take them from others; I just already had a sizable collection in my apartment, and instead of giving them out to first responders, I put them in a decorative bowl on my coffee table.

Article VII. I'm at least three months behind changing the water filter in my Keurig coffee maker.

Article VIII. I'm, like, five months behind changing the filter in my vacuum cleaner.

Article IX. While working my first job, serving ice cream at Dairy Queen in the late '90s, I often encouraged and participated in after-hours contests among me and my colleagues to see who could make the tallest ice-cream cone. We each took turns swirling large amounts onto a cone and laughing until the person with the highest cone was declared the winner. We often threw out the full cones, creating an inexcusable waste of delicious soft-serve product. Apologies to management and the nation.

Article X. In my first memoir, I alluded to the fact that my favorite ice-cream flavor is coffee. While I do very much enjoy coffee-flavored ice cream, my favorite flavor is, in fact, mint chocolate chip. I don't know what I was thinking.

𝕬rticle 𝖃𝕴. In 2021, I was sent a box of promotional swag celebrating the release of Barbra Streisand's album *Release Me 2*, which included a handwritten thank-you note from my Lordess and Savior Herself, Barbra Joan Streisand. It read, "For R—XO, B" in ultra-fine-point black ink. As of the 2024 writing of this chapter, that note has still not been professionally framed; it remains safely in the box under my bed. In my defense, I've been really busy, and—you know what? There is no acceptable defense for this.

𝕬rticle 𝖃𝕴𝕴. In my senior year of high school, I skipped multiple final exams to rehearse for the senior musical.

𝕬rticle 𝖃𝕴𝕴𝕴. Per a confession made earlier in this book, I once stole nail polish and lip gloss from my pretend-girlfriend's makeup Caboodle.

𝕬rticle 𝖃𝕴𝖁. Per another confession made earlier in this book, in my misguided effort to resolve my own daddy issues, I have hooked up with a large number of self-identifying "straight men" on the down-low, many of whom were presumably actual fathers. Really . . . there were many of them. If you live in New York and are reading this now, I may very well have hooked up with your father. In fact, if you are from anywhere in or around the Tri-State area, there is a fairly good chance that I am your mother. I don't exactly know how that would work out logistically, but please accept my sincere apologies.

𝕬rticle 15. I don't know Roman numerals after 14.

𝕬rticle 16. I was once at a function also attended by *Friends* star David Schwimmer. He was drinking a beverage from a plastic cup (it was not a great function), and after he placed the empty cup on the table next to me and walked away, my friend shielded me with her coat while I picked it up and placed it in my murse. To this day, it remains in a special place in my kitchen cabinet.

Article 17. I like to sit down when I pee. I can assure you that this is usually never an issue—unless the urinal is in a public restroom.

Article 18. While I am the target demographic, I have never seen the movie *Love, Actually*.

Article 19. ~~I organized the January 6 Capitol insurrection~~ I don't always wipe down the treadmill in my building's fitness center after I use it.

Article 20. I have never changed the filter in my vacuum cleaner.

18

WHERE DO TROLLS COME FROM?

Gather 'round, little shits, and I'll give you the scoop
On a truly unpleasant and godawful group
Oh, they're just vile creatures; they barely have souls
You guessed it: I'm speaking of Internet trolls

They lurk in our comments and slide in our DMs
And delve in our business from a.m.'s to p.m.'s
They love to provoke, and they love to berate
But the thing that they love most of all is to hate

There's nothing but spiders and crud in their hearts
They don't have a face, and they smell like their farts
They hide from the light, and they never go out
They feed on our innermost fear and self-doubt

A few are just bots, Russian state-sponsored gremlins
They spread lots of lies; their agenda's the Kremlin's
But most of these trolls are real humans—it's true
In fact, there's a chance you might be a troll too!

Do you even know where these creatures come from?
If your answer is no, a troll might call you dumb

There are so many horrible trolls with no faces
Of all different kinds and from all different places

Some trolls know it all, and they just love to tell you
Their negative comments will often repel you
They hijack your joy just to make themselves known
And correct all opinions that don't match their own

Down in a cesspool of gloom and dismay
Where they all truly know no one cares what they say
In a swamp of small-mindedness mixed with humdrum
That's where those Internet trolls all come from

Some trolls are just bullies; they bluster and bark
They frighten and threaten and bait you with snark
They slink through the Wi-Fi for which their moms paid
And torment the world 'cause they'll never get laid

Under a boulder of low self-esteem
In the shame and regret of each slimy wet dream
Where they sleep on a cot in a personal hell
That's where those Internet trolls tend to dwell

Some trolls occupy the political space
Most don't have a soul, but some do have a face
Some trolls are bright orange; some trolls are pure Greene
Some trolls get elected (you know what I mean?)

From narcissism, greed, revenge, and fake news
From misinformation and crimes they excuse
While cheating the sadly depraved and forlorn
That's where those Internet trolls are all born

Some trolls are disguised as your friends, but they're not
They're passive-aggressive and judge you a lot
"I love you, but you've put on weight," they might post
They say they support you but hate you the most

Deep in a ditch filled with no real success
Behind all of their miserable phony BS
Where the thickest resentment and envy collide
That's where those Internet trolls all reside

So how can we stop them? I hear you inquire
With garlic and sun like we would a vampire?
Should we pray they get lost in an Internet glitch?
Or melt them like Dorothy did to that witch?

We know where they come from; that part now seems clear
But how do we make all those creeps disappear?
What do trolls hate the most? What might give *them* a fright?
What's a hideous Internet troll's kryptonite?

The truth is, there's one way to make a troll break
It isn't a crucifix or wooden stake
It's no silver bullet or stone that you throw
It isn't a glitch, and it's not H_2O

It's not to encourage or incentivize
It isn't ten thousand indignant replies
It isn't to fight or defend or refute
It's not the BLOCK button or even the MUTE

If you find some trolls in the broad light of day
Just hold up a mirror and point it their way

That's right! It's that simple! And for full effect
Then pause for a moment to let them reflect

Let them see their nonfaces and smell their own farts
Show them all of the hate that they hold in their hearts
And just watch as they gaze with regret and disgust
Till they splinter and crack and they crumble to dust

Then you'll see what I mean, and you'll know that I'm right
When I tell you a troll is its own kryptonite
For the truth, where an Internet troll never delves
Is there's nothing those trolls hate as much as themselves

19

A Dear John to Social Media

Dear Social Media,

I'm sorry, but I don't think I can do this anymore. I've tried for over two decades to make it work with us, but our relationship has now grown toxic, and I think it would be best for me to move on.

I'm grateful for all you've done for me, but I'm losing myself in you. I've become so consumed with sharing my every thought, my every action, my every pricey crab-dip appetizer that I've forgotten what it all really means. Things that once brought me joy are now just empty vessels in the hollow sea of other people's approval, floating on an endless quest for clicks and likes. That's no way to exist. Don't get mad, but I feel like I want to start dating my real life again, at least casually. I miss it. I know I've broken up with you in the past, but this time I made it official with a self-important, holier-than-thou Instagram post telling people I would be taking a break from you. I just checked, and it already has over sixty-seven likes, so I fear there's no turning back this time. The world is watching.

When we first met, I had just opened an account on Friendster. God, we were just kids then; so young, so naive. I really believed all those strangers you introduced me to were my friends. It was such a fresh rush of deliciously superficial connection. I was finally "getting out there and meeting new people" like my mother had always pushed for me to do, but without the displeasure and inconvenience of actually having to meet people or go out. All my introvert prayers had been answered. Then, thanks to the influence of your old pal Ashton Kutcher, things really started heating up between us in 2009. It was fun and new. It was romantic. Everything was so easy. Now, being with you just feels like sheer drudgery . . . a never-ending chore. You need so much more from me than I'm able to give you.

I can't trust you anymore. You're too fickle, too impulsive. I need to focus on my career, and I just don't feel like I have your support. I spent years building my brand on Facebook only for you to turn around and decide all my hard-earned followers weren't cool anymore. How do you think that made me feel? Then I finally get my Twitter off the ground and, on a whim, you let a maniacal space-nerd billionaire turn it into a politically controversial rage-fueled hellscape. It's not even called Twitter anymore. I don't even know what to call it. It's just an X. And as far as you're concerned, now so am I.

I can't help but question your intentions in all this. What do you want from me now? More TikTok videos? How long can I count on *that*? Do you know that I have a meeting with my fancy digital media agent today at 1 p.m. to discuss boosting my TikTok numbers, and our lunatic Congress has a meeting one hour later to try to ban TikTok as a national security threat? This is insanity. I need stability in my life, and clearly you can't offer that. How do you expect me to plan a future with you when our entire relationship is built on a foundation of quicksand? PS, are you seriously leaking my shit to China?

I miss my independence. I resent that I need you so much. The stress of having to rely on all your goddamn platforms is keeping me awake at night. If one of them goes down, even for an hour, I feel like my entire identity is lost. What if they were all to just go away one day? In the blink of an eye, all my friends and I would no longer be life coaches, gurus, or professional models. I cannot live in that uncertainty, always at the mercy of Meta. I need to go find myself. I've been to Zuckerberg, but I've never been to me.

The screen time feature on my iPhone thinks I've been spending way too much time with you, and honestly, it's not wrong. I can't keep scrolling like this. There's no room left—in my head or my heart. My tiny human brain was not built to constantly process such a wide-ranging avalanche of information all at once: *the war in Ukraine, Timothée Chalamet and Kylie Jenner in matching tracksuits, somebody's grandmother just died, random girl doing a Jennifer Coolidge impression, Kanye West's latest apology, random hot dude doing a cold plunge, baby ducks being rescued from a storm drain to an Adele song, Kanye West rescinding his latest apology. . . .* This is a roller coaster I am not prepared to ride every day for the rest of my life. I am emotionally exhausted, and my thumb hurts.

Please, let me go . . . Set me free!

Release me from the feelings of inadequacy and sadness I take with me every time I leave you. I don't want to compare myself to other people anymore. You're constantly reminding me that I don't do enough, that I'm not good enough. I cannot compete with Taylor Swift. I will never be her. And I'm not starting a new business, no matter how much Gary Vee yells at me. I'm too tired and lazy to even start the new season of *Love Is Blind* on Netflix; a new business is highly unlikely.

Liberate me from having to read the cringey, forced, hypercasual ads and headlines posted on you by every brand and news outlet (even the most prestigious) that now thinks the way to drive traffic and seem relatable is to adopt the written tone of a fourteen-year-old who watches too much *RuPaul's Drag Race* and has a blog: *Besties, we are so shook by the smackdown Hillary Clinty just served the GOP, we literally can't even! Smash the link in our bio because we are spilling all that yummy tea, mama!*

Why are they talking like that? They're *The New York Times*.

Free me from the zombie fog I walk around in all day as the result of your unrelenting distractions. All your pings and notifications have left me so cognitively impaired that sometimes I can't sit through an entire ten-word meme, let alone a full-length feature film. I miss my precious attention span.

I've had enough of all the noise—figurative and literal. You've become an endless barrage of people screaming into the Internet: LOOK AT ME, LOOK AT ME . . . ! STOP SCROLLING . . . ! GET READY WITH ME . . . ! WATCH ME, WATCH ME, NOTICE ME, WATCH ME . . . ! Everyone is so terrified of not being heard above all the noise that all they do is yell at their audience. It's like suddenly everyone is Crazy Eddie. Remember Crazy Eddie, the electronics chain that had those annoying commercials in the '80s with that guy (Crazy Eddie) who talked really fast like he was on coke and was always yelling that his "PRICES ARE INSAAAANE"? I think it was just a Northeast thing. Anyway, I'm sure you can look it up. You're social media. Where was I? Oh, yeah . . .

Give me back my attention span! Also, enough with the Jennifer Coolidge impressions. Even the really strong ones all sound exactly the same.

I am done participating in every one of your inane challenges, hashtags, and trends: *Do the latest dance. . . . Buy the newest foundation. . . . Eat a box of dishwasher detergent. . . . Post a picture from your first abortion. . . .* Why do we always have to do what *you* want to do? Can't I have an original thought?

I am sick and tired of your infinite stream of negativity. Did you know that because of you, the average human currently absorbs in one day what would have been considered a lifetime's worth of tragedy twenty-five years ago? I have been so conditioned to expect only the worst news from you that I can no longer scroll past a picture of a celebrity without assuming that celebrity has died.

I don't recognize you anymore. You're hateful and bigoted sometimes. You used to be nice. You won't like me saying this, but it's because of you that psychopathic morons are being elected to the most powerful positions and the worst of humanity is mobilizing to wreak havoc on society. I remember the good old days, when the scariest thing about the Internet was the dial-up sound my modem made every time it connected to AOL. Look at what you've done.

Lies and misinformation are everywhere, and it's all because of you. As we navigate these precarious times, rife with deception and distortions of the truth, there is nothing more dangerous than misinformation. I remember reading an article in *Teen People* back in 1999 that quoted Justin Timberlake as saying he believed that "even one stray eyebrow could ruin an entire look." In hindsight, I'm pretty sure JT never really said that, but it sure did lead to my severe overplucking well into the late aughts. I don't ever want to go back there again, and that is why I have to say Bye Bye Bye.

There may come a time in the future when I'm ready to give you another chance (probably tomorrow morning, if not later this afternoon). For now, though, I ask that you please give me MySpace and allow me this much-needed pause to work on my mental health. And my Jennifer Coolidge impression.

Sincerely signing off (for now),

Randy

20

From the Peanut Gallery

I know the rule is that we're never supposed to respond to negative comments. They say feeding trolls only gives them the power they so wretchedly crave. Truth be told, I rarely even look at comments anymore. For my money, everyone's gotten just a tad too comfy exposing the vilest parts of themselves. Of course, some comments are very kind, but they're simply not worth having to sift through all that toxic sludge. Even many of the well-intentioned ones can misfire and instantly send me spiraling into a days-long depression.

Between you and me, I think people who leave negative comments are more deranged than people who travel recreationally. And I know what you're thinking: *Oh, so Princess Randy is allowed to dish out a bunch of complaints and opinions about stuff, but the second somebody gives it back a little, suddenly he's too precious?* That's absolutely correct. Furthermore, I may have tons of negative comments to share about lots of things, but I would never dream of giving them away on other people's social media platforms. I wait until someone offers to pay me, and then I dump them all in a book. It's called "literature."

To that point, I hope you won't mind if I use this opportunity to catch up a bit on my correspondence (and also generate some

content). Many of my adoring fans have been waiting months—
some even years—to hear back from me, and I thought I'd reply
to some of them now. Normally I'd just send autographed eight-
by-ten headshots, but why not save myself a few stamps and let my
publisher foot the bill?

*Note: All of the below comments are real, but most commenters'
names have been slightly altered to protect the obnoxious.*

From: SexyPatriot87

Posted on Twitter (or whatever that's called now)

**"Is this guy's voice for real like that or does he just doing that
to sound gay?"**

Dear Sexy,

Thanks so much for your question. I was able to decode it with an
app on my phone that converts unintelligible mishmash into properly constructed sentences. The answer, I'm relieved to tell you, is
that your astute speculation is correct. I affect this phony gay voice
only for professional reasons. My agents and I find it helps get me
a lot of work in more mainstream arenas. My real voice is about
three octaves lower, somewhere in Demi Moore's register. It's all
just showbiz, my friend . . . sort of like how your username suggests
that you might in any way be sexually appealing (I've seen the profile
pic).

Buckets of love,

Randy

From: Susan Batschlitz
Posted on Facebook

"You have a beautiful facial profile, Randy. Every time you turn your head, I notice your beautiful jawline. You should show your profile more! Much better than the front."

Dear Susan,

Thank you for your kind words. I was so sad to see them end before you stopped typing. I truly admire your ability to express yourself so freely without burden of consideration for how other people might feel after you've done so. As soon as I get out of my bed, which, thanks to your comment, will be roughly three weeks from today, I will take your advice and present myself publicly only at a 90-degree angle. Going forward, if I must be front-facing for any reason—be it a Zoom call, a live stage appearance, or the missionary position during lovemaking—I will be sure to put a paper bag over my head.

Thanks again!
Hugs from every direction,
Randy

From: JackLong44
Posted on Instagram

"I'm unfollowing you."

Dear Jack,

Thank you for the heads-up. I'll have my attorney send over the appropriate paperwork. You can keep the silverware.

Hit the road,
Randy

From: Jenny Paroo

Posted on Instagram

"We love your parody videos in our house, but please use more contemporary songs. My daughter is thirteen and doesn't know *The Music Man* or *Oklahoma!*"

Dear Jenny,

So glad to hear from you! Bringing families closer together is something I strive to do, so I love that you're watching with your darling daughter. Perhaps now would be a perfect time to explain to the little brat that this planet actually existed before she graced it with her divine presence. She might find the concept bewildering at first, but stick with it and maybe she'll get it eventually.

I myself was not even close to being born when *The Music Man* originally opened on Broadway in 1957 (and thanks for noticing). In fact, my mother was barely out of kindergarten at the time. Still, my curiosity as a young person led me to discover it through ancient relics known as records, books, and conversation. I'm all the more cultured and enriched now as a result, and I wish the same for your spawn. I enjoy a lot of contemporary music and, in fact, pay tribute to it frequently in my work. I also enjoy the idea of encouraging today's youth to embrace interests that lie beyond the palms of their own sweaty little hands. Just because it's not on TikTok doesn't necessarily mean it belongs rotting in a dumpster or that it isn't worthy of occupying space in their tiny, overcrowded minds. Just a thought!

Thanks again for watching, and love to your daughter. She sounds awful.

Shipoopi,
Randy

From: Jared Parsons

Posted on Amazon.com (book review of my memoir *Playing with Myself*)

"Too many words. Gave me a headache."

Dear Jared,

Well, you're certainly anything but long-winded. And I agree with you . . . books are no place for words. In my defense, I did originally pitch a textless photo book of my most tasteful nudes, but the publisher rejected the idea. Sorry for the headache.

R

Note: This next (very real) comment came from the social media account belonging to a high-profile elected official (at least she still is at the time of this writing), so her identity will not be concealed.

From: laurenboebert

Posted on Twitter (or whatever)

"We went from Reading Rainbow to Randy Rainbow in a few decades, but don't dare say the left is grooming our kids!"

Dear Lauren,

Well, this is a treat! I had no idea you were a fan. Of course, it's been well-publicized that you like bringing dates to family-friendly musicals, so I suppose it tracks. Still, I know you've got your . . . hands full over there, so thanks for . . . reaching out. I also had no idea that I was heir apparent to the great LeVar Burton, but I'll take it! Actually, I can't stand kids and I'm not a big reader, so I wouldn't be overly concerned if I were you (unless, of course, we're talking about job security). I'm not really one for grooming other people in general, but if I could offer any guidance in that department, I'd probably start with your split ends. Also, bigotry and homophobia haven't been fashionable for years, gurl. Don't you remember all that *Let he who is without sin . . .* jazz? Take a look; it's in a book.

> Sincerely your favorite
> butterfly in the sky,
> Randy Rainbow

From: TomV896

Posted on **YouTube**

"OMG your amazing!"

Dear Tom,

I'm sadly unable to accept this compliment due to your egregious spelling error.

> You'res truly,
> Randy

From: **Larry Campbell**

Posted on **Ticketmaster.com (review of my live concert)**

"Not political enough. Too much singing."

Dear Larry,

You're absolutely right. I'll work on that.

> XO,
> Randy

[1]

From: Gretchen L.

Posted on Ticketmaster.com (review of my live concert)

"Too political! Stick to musical comedy."

Dear Gretchen,

You're absolutely right. I'll work on that.

XO,
Randy

From: datfatasss4u

Sent via Grindr

"Dude if ur gonna catfish at least use a pic of Henry Cavill, lol. You ain't gonna lure insuspecting [*sic*] gays with Rainbow Randy. PS, if u really Rainbow Randy let's grab a drink."

Dear Mr. Dat Fat,

Thank you so much for your insightful counsel. I will take it under advisement the next time I fish for cats. I appreciate your cocktail invitation, but I'd hate to lure you *un*suspectingly only to disappoint. Thanks anyway.

Sincerely,
Henry Cavill

From: JulieCat424

Posted on Instagram

"Where are you?! Why haven't you been posting? Are you dead???"

Hey, Julie!

Thank you for your hostile concern, total stranger. Contrary to your dramatic assumption, the fact that you haven't seen me pop up on Instagram for a while does not necessarily mean I have passed away. In fact, the more infrequently I post, the busier I usually am. I might be touring, writing, recording . . . whatever it is I'm doing, rest assured that it's most likely exactly what I need or want to be doing. I promise to return with fresh new content for you just as soon as I'm ready and able to do so. Unless of course I am dead . . . then it might take a little longer.

Alive and well, Randy

From: Linda Warshavsky

Posted to Amazon.com (book review for my memoir *Playing with Myself*)

"Bad language! It was interesting but I could not get past the terrible language, swearing, F word."

Dear Linda,

I had no idea my audience was so puritanical. I guess I did drop a fair amount of F-bombs in that book (as I do in real life), but it was hardly the screenplay to *Scarface*. Was it really bad enough to warrant a two-star rating? Despite your perception that generous swearing is rude or lowbrow, I've actually read articles that say it may be a sign of intelligence and verbal superiority. I've also read conflicting articles that say it may be a sign of dementia. I choose to believe the former. In any event, I doubt you'll like this book any better. Maybe I'm just not your cup of tea!

With shits and giggles,
Randy Fucking Rainbow

From: FernThompson2

Sent via Instagram direct message

"Randy, I think you are a great takent [*sic*]. I loved watching your stories etc. But randy your constant postings are much too much. Got burnt out on you quickly and finally decided to mute your postings & stories! What do you think that says about you? I'm sure I'm not the only one."

Dearest Fern,

What can I say? I had never really looked inward until after reading your DM. I am now so ashamed. Had I realized the unthinkable turmoil I was causing you with my three posts per week at most, I would have gotten the help I needed much sooner. I notice you only follow six other people (three more than follow you). Were I a brilliant scientist, I might identify that as the reason you're experiencing my totally average posting schedule as an aggressive bombardment, but I'm sure you're right and that it's actually the residual abandonment issues from my childhood. How wise you are, Fern. You have a real "takent" for getting to the heart of things. Thank you for your intervention. To spare you any further distress, I will now block you on my end.

All the best,
Randy

PS (with apologies to Linda Warshavsky): Fuck off, Fern.

21

Don't Panic, It's Just My Face

Oh, hello. You must be my airport greeter. Although I guess since I've been waiting here at the terminal entrance for you since my driver dropped me off eight minutes ago, I'm technically *your* airport greeter. That's what I'd like to say to you, but I won't because that would be rude. More to the point, I'm afraid if I did, you might tweet about it—or X about it, or queef about it, or whatever we're doing now—and tell people that I'm rude. I'm not really a rude person. At least I don't think I'm rude. I'm just really tired and cranky, and I generally don't like talking to people. Maybe I *am* a rude person.

You, on the other hand, are definitely not a rude person; at least you certainly don't seem to think you are. For example, you kept me waiting here for eight minutes and twenty-four seconds and haven't even apologized for it. What I mean is, you're not rude-presenting. Good for you. You are very bouncy and smiley and—oh, look at that—extremely talkative. Fuck . . . this will be miserable.

No, that's fine; no need to help me with any of these heavy bags. I'm pretty sure I already developed scoliosis while waiting for you. What's a little more destructive spinal compression?

What's that you say, now? You didn't bother to print out my boarding pass because you figured I'd have it on my phone? Perfection! I will find a free elbow to fish it out of my coat pocket or rub myself up against a wall until it eventually pops out. Or maybe I'll just . . . oh, actually, I see that I don't have time to do any of those because you are walking extremely fast. Funny, you didn't strike me as the type to rush. In fact, I need to run a little to keep up with you. No worries. I'll just clumsily plant my bags at the security desk and hold up this line of disgruntled TSA PreCheck customers you just awkwardly ushered me past a little longer. By the sounds of the profanities they're mumbling, I have a feeling they already don't care for me, so no love lost.

As I begin walking through the body scanner, I can't help but notice that the TSA agent waiting on the other side is screaming at me to take my shoes off. That's odd. They don't usually make us take off our shoes in the TSA PreCheck line. No one who can afford the extravagance of a $78-fee spanning five years would ever put anything questionable in their shoes. Oh . . . what's that you're now screaming at me in unison with the screaming TSA agent? This isn't TSA PreCheck? This airport doesn't allow greeters through the PreCheck line, so you took me through the regular TSA line instead? Hmm. What an ironic burden. No, it's totally fine. I actually prefer less convenience for more money. I didn't cough up the extra $200 for this service to enjoy any of the time-saving benefits it offers, let alone the ones I already pay for. I just really wanted to meet you and show you my new socks.

I notice you're not wearing an official uniform. There's really nothing official-looking about you. I see no airline logo or anything emblematic of the aviation industry, for that matter, anywhere on your attire (and by now, I'm searching). By all appearances, you're just an aggressive person whom no one working at this airport seems to recognize or acknowledge professionally. Who are you? It's too early and I'm too tired to stop you from kidnapping me if that's what's happening. I'm just interested. Actually, I'm not that interested. Carry on.

Now we're walking to the airline's lounge. I'm still the only one of us carrying my bags. However, any discomfort or aggravation I might be feeling is dulled by the distraction of having to pretend I'm at all interested as you begin to regale me with historical facts about this airport. No, I had no idea it was home to the fourteenth-largest FedEx hub in the world or that they filmed a scene for *Buffy the Vampire Slayer* here in 1998. I really just want to get to North Carolina so that I can do my show and get back home to my cat and my toilet.

After your third time asking, I finally convince you that I'm not hungry and don't plan to eat anything here. You reward me by not asking for a fourth time. What did I eat before I came, you ask? I got back to my hotel room at 11:30 last night and didn't fall asleep until 2 a.m. before having to wake up at 2:45 a.m. to drive to this piece-of-shit airport in this godforsaken city with only one airport . . . I've had no opportunity to develop an appetite. This is more information than I care to share with you, and again, I might sound rude if I do, so instead I just say, "Grape-Nuts." Thankfully, this is an acceptable answer, and you allow us to move on.

We arrive at the VIP section of the lounge. There's nothing that visibly distinguishes it from any other section. I only know it's the VIP section because you yell, "THIS IS THE VIP SECTION!" at an elderly couple sitting there and force them to relocate so that I can sit there instead. I try to stop you, but it's too late. Everyone in this lounge is now giving me dirty looks. Thankfully, I never plan to visit this city again.

You tell me I have about an hour before boarding. I begin to thank you and say that I'll see you again in an hour but then notice you taking a seat next to me. I see. You plan to sit here with me for the entire hour. This is really happening. All I want to do is shout, "THIS IS THE VIP SECTION!" at you until you leave, but instead, I swallow my deep despair and smile a giant smile. I casually open the Google app on my phone and search how long it would take to walk to North Carolina.

I'm a little dead inside after two-and-a-half minutes of polite conversation about the weather, but you—you're just warming up. Now you're ready to take our relationship to the next level. You finally disclose that you're familiar with my work. You're a big fan, you say? That is so wonderful, and under any other circumstances, I would be so very honored by your accolades. Under these circumstances, I hate you. I don't really hate you. I just hate airports at 5 a.m.

You're halfway through a story about your nephew's graduation when it happens. My fatigued, artificial grin begins to crumble and finally defaults to my underlying RBF, or "resting bitch face," as it's known medically. You are startled. Your labored exterior cracks briefly, revealing a glimpse of the sad and beautiful frailty dwelling within. You have discovered the painful truth we have both been trying to deny all along: that I don't give a shit about your nephew's graduation. I can tell you're starting to panic. Please don't panic! This is just what my face looks like when I'm not concealing my true feelings of general disinterest in almost everything and everyone!

You're still panicking.

My borderline codependent empathic personality disorder kicks in. Now I must rescue you from your emotions and my face. Oh, why was I cursed with this affliction of basic human kindness? Our only hope now is for me to slide into high gear and deploy every last drop of energy I can muster. My face becomes overly animated. My leg crosses over my thigh and my thumb comes up under my chin as I lean in toward you, feigning curiosity. I begin to ask you dozens of follow-up questions about your nephew's graduation and follow up with an amusing anecdote about my own nephew. I do not have a nephew, but in a desperate effort to connect with you in this moment, I give myself one. I'm perky and gesturing enthusiastically with my hands. Everyone around us is now noticing what a good time we're having. Even the elderly couple you yelled at seems a bit sadder that they were bounced from the VIP section. Suddenly, I'm holding court. I'm charming; I'm funny; I'm delightful; I'm fully depleted of my life force. I will definitely have to cancel my show in North Carolina.

By now, I'm making a mental note to add an item to my rider specifying that no greeters are to sit with me at the airport. Ugh . . . that sounds so bitchy, though. I would hate for my travel agent or anyone on my team to think I'm a diva. Fortunately, I remember that nobody ever reads my rider, so it should be safe.

The hour is finally up, and it's time to make our way. No, I don't need to use the restroom, but thank you for your concern. Yes, there's no need to help me with my heavy bags, and thank you for your consistency. I didn't pay the extra $200 for any of the useful luggage or ticketing assistance this service falsely advertises; I'm just a professional adult who really wanted a babysitter to monitor my breakfast habits and remind me to make pee-pee before the airplane goes bye-bye.

Once at the gate, you whisk me past a row of wheelchair-bound grandparents, nearly knocking over three pregnant women and trampling an entire platoon of disabled Vietnam veterans so that I can board first. I am officially the most hated VIP in this or any airport. At this point, I don't think they'd let me back into this city if I tried.

You direct me to my seat on the plane, pointing to a spot in the overhead bin where I can put my bags. I thank you for what I assume was meant to be your help and tell you it was a pleasure meeting you as the dark cloud of this experience begins to slowly lift. At long last, you are out of sight, and I have once again reclaimed my glorious independence. A wave of gratitude washes over me. I am completely exhausted, physically and emotionally. It's only 6 a.m.

22

And While We're on the Subject . . .

Uh-oh! It looks like I'm getting the red light! That can mean only one of two things: either we're quickly nearing the end of this book, or it's time for me to go to my other job, moonlighting as a high-class hooker in the Garment District. I have a feeling it's not the latter (I'm off today), so I'll try to use my remaining time with you wisely, America. I know I've lodged a lot of complaints here, and yet not nearly as many as I would have liked. So allow me to squeeze in a few more pet peeves, irks, irritants, annoyances, and grievances (in no particular order) . . .

Handshaking: May we finally put this hideous practice to rest, once and for all? I thought maybe we had, but it seems to be more prevalent than ever. Don't take offense, but I never want to touch your disgusting hand. I'm a germophobe. Please find a more suitable way of greeting me, like applauding.

Public spitting: Why are people constantly spitting? It seems to happen everywhere I go. Maybe I should start taking it personally. All kinds of people: businessmen, brides, butchers, bakers, candlestick-makers . . . they just spit all over the place! On the sidewalks, into garbage cans, on the subway, out their car windows . . . I have gone my entire life without ever experiencing a sudden need to expectorate in any public setting, and I expect the same of you. If this is not the case, please seek medical care immediately.

People who get way too excited about becoming an uncle or aunt: Calm down. It's not a Kennedy Center Honor.

People who pronounce the word "aunt" like "ont": It's pronounced "ant" like the insect, fancy-pants. What is this—*Downton Abbey?*

Those automated "CAPTCHA" tests that pop up on websites to deter spam bots and make you prove you're a human by solving puzzles: I'm a fucking human. Just let me pay for the shitty sunglasses you've succeeded in tricking me into purchasing from your sketchy website, whoever-you-are. I don't have time to find all the fire hydrants. I have things to do. I shouldn't even be on your website right now. I've frankly never heard of your brand. I don't even know how I got here. I clicked on some random Instagram link when you hypnotized me with your evil ad-targeting witchcraft. For all I know, I may have been drugged. I'm the one who should be taking extra precautions here—not you. Yet here I am, eagerly prepared to supply you with all of my credit-card information just because you asked me to, only not until I find all the fire hydrants.

I'm not a preschooler—I shouldn't have to spend nine minutes of my day looking for fire hydrants. And yes, that's how long it takes because I never complete the task on the first, second, or even fourth try. If you're going to treat me like a preschooler, at least use clear, simplistic illustrations of fire hydrants that a preschooler might recognize, not grainy iPhone pictures that were apparently taken by some drunken spring-breaker in Cancun. Who the fuck can decipher a fire hydrant from anything else in these pictures? *Is that the top of a fire hydrant or somebody's thumb? I think this one might be a fire hydrant, but hard to tell with that huge rock in front of it . . . or is that a dead body?* I don't want to go through this every time I buy something I don't need or want online, which is at least eight times a day. Please just steal all of my money already, and then go find the fire hydrants yourself.

People who tell me to "have a safe flight": Sweetie, I'm not flying the plane. When someone sits in the audience to watch a Broadway show, do you tell them to "break a leg"? When you finish dining at a restaurant, do you tip the patrons sitting at the table next to you and compliment them on how delicious your chicken cacciatore was? I appreciate the sentiment, but it's completely misguided.

People wearing any kind of sandal or open-toed shoe who absolutely should not: You know who you are, folks. If you take away only one lesson from this book, please let it be this: Flip-flops are a privilege, not a right.

Camera technology on iPhones getting progressively more high-definition as I progressively do not get any younger: That's quite enough, Tim Cook. I don't need to see every single pore, nor do I have hours to spend on the amount of retouching now necessary to post a single picture of me and my friends. Every prefiltered selfie I've taken beyond the iPhone 8 Plus has been an assault. Bring back the soft-focus of 2012, and let us return to the willful ignorance we once enjoyed before you started showing us what we actually look like.

People who are younger than I am: The unmitigated gall . . .

People who are older than I am but look younger than I am: This upsets me even more. Enough is enough, Lenny Kravitz.

The voice dictation feature on my iPhone: Why does my phone never understand a word I say? I've always prided myself on having immaculate diction. After all, I'm a classically trained opera singer. I mean, I'm not really, but I tell people I am. The point is, *I* can always understand exactly what I'm saying as I'm saying it, and yet the words that appear in text messages and emails I dictate to my iPhone never match. Apparently I have some unintelligible speech impediment or thick Irish brogue that I was completely unaware of until I started using this feature.

That other version of "Somewhere Over the Rainbow": Hawaiian musician Israel Kamakawiwo'ole's recording of the song (which is perfectly lovely) has arguably become more popular than any of Judy Garland's versions. I have a problem with this on its own, but to make matters worse, he sings the wrong lyrics! It's not even subtle, and it happens almost immediately: Instead of "Somewhere over the rainbow, way up high, there's a land that I heard of," he sings, "Somewhere over the rainbow, way up high, and the dreams that you dream of once in a lullaby." Huh? That puzzling non sequitur appears nowhere in Harold Arlen's original song. But wait . . . there's more! He then, in the very next verse, goes on to sing, ". . . bluebirds fly, and the dreams that you dream of—dreams really do come true." Not only does that make no sense, it doesn't rhyme! The official clip has over one billion views on YouTube, compared to Judy's fifty-three million. Can we not get him in studio for a quick rerecord? I mean, what's the holdup?

Addendum to my previous comments: I just googled, and Israel Kamakawiwo'ole is sadly no longer with us. He passed away in 1997. My condolences.

Self-taped auditions: Please stop subjecting me to the abject cringe of this cruel and degrading humiliation. Just give me all of the parts, and let's call it a day.

The fact that my Cetaphil Gentle Skin Cleanser looks so much like human semen: Guys, I'm pretty sure it's just semen.

"Breaking news": Didn't "breaking news" once mean news that is breaking—as in something that just happened or is currently happening? It's not still "Breaking News" if you reported it over twelve hours ago; it's already quite broken. Cool it with the dramatic bumpers! They're not meant to be used after every single commercial break! They should be reserved for special occasions, just like fancy bar soaps, expensive dinnerware, or anal beads.

Also, there's too much creative writing in political journalism these days. The facts are horrifying enough on their own. We can do without the excessive hyperbole. Please refrain from overuse of adjectives like "major," "bombshell," and "explosive." Love you, Wolf Blitzer . . . but chill, bro. The only thing "breaking" is my TV screen when I throw my half-empty bottle of Tito's at it, and the only thing "explosive" is the diarrhea you're giving me from all this breaking news.

Chronic illness commercials with super-catchy jingles: Some of these songs are straight-up amazing bops, and it's starting to interfere with my day. I wish you all the best in managing your ulcerative colitis and Crohn's disease, but I don't need to randomly start singing about it in the cereal aisle at Whole Foods.

Con Edison drilling outside my apartment for the last three months: What the hell are they searching for . . . a ConEd customer service representative? Good luck, because I have yet to locate one.

Overly produced talk shows: I'm a huge fan of talk shows, but nowadays, they're generally overproduced, in my opinion. Except, of course, for the ones I will be appearing on to promote this book—those are perfect. Please let us return to the days of genuine, relaxed, intelligent conversation (I so miss that on television), and knock it off with all the cutesy games and gimmicks. Don't put Dame Judi Dench through the torment of enduring three rounds of Celebrity Beer Pong Karaoke opposite Carrot Top just so that you can have a viral clip the next morning. The woman's a goddamn national treasure.

People who say "You look tired" and have no idea what they're saying is wildly offensive: These people are terrorists.

Farmhouse-style sinks in bathrooms: Why is this so popular in modern decor? Every five-star-hotel bathroom sink is a square. The tight corners and flat-bottom basin of this design are completely impractical when shaving or teeth-brushing. I'm always left having to manually usher my own spit-up toothpaste down the drain like it's an elderly person trying to find their seat at a Sunday matinee. How is this a luxury experience?

Mario Lopez constantly appearing on every hotel-room TV: Is no one else available? I like Mario Lopez, but it's evident that even he doesn't want to be there, trapped inside my Marriott television screen, promoting movies he's never seen and never plans to see. I can just tell he doesn't give two shits about the musical film adaptation of *The Color Purple*. What I'm trying to say is, I think it's time for new leadership, and I would like to officially throw my hat in the ring.

People who put me on speakerphone: I honestly don't have the time, energy, or space to address those people right now. I will need to write an entirely separate book.

Trailers for movie musicals that include precisely zero singing: Movie musicals are back in the mainstream, which is a wonderful thing! The genre is obviously commercially viable enough for studios to spend millions on production, and yet they still find it necessary to trick moviegoers into seeing them by concealing their true identities when marketing them. Shit or get off the pot, Hollywood! I know there are paying customers who might be turned off by power-belting and too much choreography in a coming attraction . . . eff those people! I think I speak for true theater nerds everywhere when I say that we ain't lookin' for no Johnny-come-latelies. I know it's a gamble, but you're either with us or against us, Hollywood! If you don't love us at our *Cats* (2019), then you don't deserve us at our *La La Land*.

Long-ass paper receipts: Did you know it takes the wood of three giant sequoias to produce one of my receipts from Sephora?

Paper straws: I'm all for saving the planet and supporting marine wildlife through renewable resources, but this is one instance in which Mother Nature can literally kiss my ecofriendly ass. There is nothing more upsetting or unappealing than having to suck my nine-dollar Starbucks through a cardboard tube. I'm environmentally responsible to a point, but I draw the line here. Watch out, endangered sea turtles! Mama's never lettin' go of her plastic straws.

Time changes of any kind: When I am president, I will finally put an end to all clock inequality and inconsistency. This means no more daylight-saving nonsense (the sun will always set sensibly at 6 p.m.; it has no business being out after I've had my first cocktail of the evening) and no more multiple time zones. Here's the truth (and I'm not afraid to say it): Eastern Standard Time is the actual time. It just is. Pacific Time, Central Time, Mountain Time . . . those are all bullshit. Alaska Time is definitely not a real thing. It's very simple, folks: I live in New York, and so that's what time it is. Please adjust your devices accordingly.

Jonathan Groff: We get it—you're perfect—whatever. (I love you; call me.)

Public nose-blowing, coughing, and sneezing: Not to sound harsh, but all of these deserve a minimum of two to five years in a correctional facility. Violently blowing your nose in public is never acceptable etiquette. Nose-blowing, in general, is an extremely personal and offensive practice that should be kept behind closed doors, like heterosexuality.

If you must cough or sneeze in public, at least cover your freaking mouth the proper way: into a tissue or into your elbow if you do not have a tissue. Really, though, I would prefer you just hold it in.

That said . . . ew, don't hold it in! That's gross, too! Not only is it gross, it's dangerous. Pinching your nose while sneezing puts pressure in the eustachian tubes that connect your nose to your ears and could inflict trauma on the eardrum. It could even damage blood vessels in your eyeballs! I can't stand when people do this, either. I know I can't have it all ways on this topic, so I guess what I'm trying to say is, everyone just stay home; never leave your house . . . ever.

People who use handkerchiefs as tissues: This might warrant a life sentence in a maximum-security state prison. It is completely unsanitary, and I don't know why you even need me to tell you that. You're walking around with a piece of cloth drenched in your own snot and reusing it throughout the day. You might believe this is the proper function of a handkerchief, but you are mistaken. Handkerchiefs are purely decorative accessories that should only be worn in suit-jacket pockets, tied around the neck if you're playing the role of Rizzo in a production of *Grease*, or worn on your head if you're playing the role of Chava in a production of *Fiddler on the Roof.*

Poor grammar: I'm definitely kind of a grammar nazi (by the way, the only acceptable kind of nazi in my opinion—not to be controversial). Misplaced apostrophes, dangling modifiers, and malapropisms of all kinds can often trigger me. My list of linguistic pet peeves is long, but since we don't have all day, here are just a few important highlights to which I would like to draw your attention (and thank you for noticing that I didn't end that sentence with a preposition):

1. You are "enamored *of*" something, not "enamored *with*" it. I'm taking a hard line on this.

2. There is no "s" in the word "anyway." It should never be pluralized. If you say "anyways," then you are an assholes.

3. When you protest that you "*could* care less" about something, it means there's still a chance that you may kind of care about it. If you want to effectively demonstrate what a coldhearted, aloof d-bag you are (and who doesn't on occasion?), try the correct usage and say that you "*couldn't* care less" about it. You'll be hated in no time!

4. "Irregardless" is not a word. Many dictionaries now recognize it because so many of you insist on using it that they finally caved, but REGARDLESS, it will never be a word.

5. The phrase you are trying to say is "for all intents and purposes." It is not "for all intensive purposes." It is also not "for all insects and porpoises." And it is definitely not "for all

extensive purchases." Any utterance of the phrase other than "for all intents and purposes" is what some would call a malapropism or—more accurately—an "eggcorn," which, for all incentive Percocets, just means you sound like a dummy.

I won't get into punctuation right now, but I would like to acknowledge that it was recently brought to my attention that younger generations have decided all punctuation (particularly periods, exclamation points, and question marks) is overtly aggressive and should no longer be used in any written context. I would like to apologize for my barbaric usage of those things throughout this book. Also, I would like to get off of this planet.

Reaction videos: This is a popular trend on YouTube. People film themselves watching stuff so that other people can watch them watching it. Sometimes they're watching a musical performance, sometimes a movie trailer. . . . The entire substance of these videos is people's candid reactions to other people actually doing things that are of substance. Some have tens of millions of views. This aggravates me so much that I'm almost tempted to use an exclamation point, but I would hate to offend anyone.

Children flying first-class: Sorry, parents. Keep them in coach or the overhead compartment where they belong.

People who text while they walk: I hate these people, mostly because I am them.

Bikers and bike lanes: Here's a startling statistic: Once every fifteen minutes in Manhattan, someone riding a bicycle almost violently kills me. "Maybe stop texting while you walk, schmuck," I hear you rudely saying to me, and you may have a point. However, I'm most often not at fault. I don't know what kind of ancient demon curse inhabits these public bike-share bikes, turning average New Yorkers into crazed supervillains who believe they're invincible, but we must find it and cast it out by exorcism or other spiritual means. Forget global warming—bike lanes are currently the greatest existential threat we face.

Professional male wrestling: I have never understood wrestling as a sport. Like, why not just fuck?

Automated out-of-office email replies and silenced text message notifications: Contrary to popular belief, these features do not completely absolve you of all moral and professional obligations. Don't ask me how my Aunt Gladys's hernia operation went in a text message and then immediately switch your phone to "do not disturb" mode. Don't you know I can see the little crescent moon icon at the bottom of our conversation with the notification that says "Your sucky friend who pretends to care about you has notifications silenced"?

The automated out-of-office reply feature should also be used sparingly. The OOO email, as it's commonly known, is a friendly courtesy only until it is not. It does eventually expire. There's this guy I'm doing business with (trying, anyway) whom I've been attempting to get hold of for months, but I'm still getting the same autoresponse saying he's away for Christmas and won't be reachable until after the New Year. It's currently April, so I'm starting to wonder which year he means. I'm almost positive he was fired from his job or tragically mowed down while attempting to cross a bike lane.

Movies and TV shows that are too dark: I don't mean thematically, I mean literally. Why is this the new norm? I'm all for realism, but turn on a damn light. I can't see shit.

Alexa: She's getting a little too chatty lately. I asked her a simple question the other day. She answered normally, but instead of then going back to sleep like she used to, she took the opportunity to launch her own counterinterrogation, as if to passive-aggressively say, *Oh, good, since we're doing questions, I have an agenda of my own. . . .* First she asked if I wanted to thank the driver of my last Amazon order. What is that supposed to mean? I need this robot to remind me to use basic manners like she's my mother? *What do we say to the nice man who drove all the way uptown with your condoms, Randy?* Then she suggested that I put on a sweater because it was cold out and reminded me that I was running low on paper towels and multivitamins. I just asked this bitch what time it was. Why do I suddenly feel like I'm in an assisted living facility?

And finally . . .

People who find it necessary to lick their finger before turning a page: I am generally not in favor of capital punishment; however, this is one exception.

23

Do I Hear a Schmaltz?

I would like to go out on a high note. I've done lots of complaining in this book, and I would hate for you to leave with the impression that I'm a big ol' Negative Nelly. I actually feel very positive about a lot of things. I could go on singing for days about all the fabulous wonders of the world.

Still, no matter how much lipstick we put on this pig, it's clear that we're on a path to extinction. As I type this, it's hailing in California and there are earthquakes in New York. So before we peace-out as a human race, here (in no particular order) is a brief catalog of twenty-five things I absolutely love about this life and will miss in the impending apocalypse.

1. **Seasons and holidays**
   I don't trust anyone who doesn't love the change of seasons or celebrate all holidays. These are life's colorful little bookmarks and should always be relished to the fullest.

2. **Scented candles**

3. **The view from my living room of pink-and-orange sunsets over the Manhattan skyline**
   I still can't believe that shit is free.

4. **Flavored martinis**

5. **My cat's slow blinks**
   They're her way of saying, "I love you."

6. **My Keurig coffee maker**

7. **Hot tea**
   I only recently started getting into it. I was sleeping on tea for the longest, you guys! Why did no one tell me about tea? Tea time is now my favorite time of day. I'm finally morphing into an elderly British lady, and I love it. (Currently sipping Harney & Sons Japanese Sencha.)

8. **Catherine O'Hara**
   I cannot stress this enough.

9. **The movie *Steel Magnolias***
   It might be the greatest movie of all time; required viewing at least once a year.

10. **Disney World**

11. **Strippers**

12. **Vinyl records**
    I bought a record player during the pandemic, and I'm happy to report that I haven't lost interest in it the way I did everything else I bought during the pandemic (RIP, my Nordic-Track elliptical).

13. **Jake Gyllenhaal**
    Now and forever . . .

14. **Vacuuming**

    I'm passionate about vacuuming. I don't know why, but it brings me immense joy. I remember seeing Whitney Houston interviewed once, and she talked about how much she loved to vacuum. That's something she and I have in common. That and the voice.

15. **Whitney Houston's version of "The Star-Spangled Banner"**

    No one will ever come close.

16. **Musical theater**

17. **Food-delivery services of all kinds**

18. **Dogs who run around with those hind-leg dog wheelchairs**

    It's legitimately the most inspiring and heartwarming thing.

19. **Horror movies**

20. **Appetizers**

21. **Pee-wee Herman**

    I've always loved Pee-wee Herman. About a year before Paul Reubens died, he sent me an Instagram message that said, "I'm embarrassingly late to the party of you! But I'm here now." We kept in touch after that. He would text me his favorite YouTube clips (including Ethel Merman guest-starring on an episode of *That Girl*). The Christmas card he sent me will always be a prized possession. I feel so lucky that he made it to my party. I only wish he could have stayed longer.

22. **Thomas Newman's score from *Angels in America***

23. Living alone

I really love the idea of finding a life partner with whom I could form a meaningful bond and eventually build a home that we could share in sickness and health, as long as we both shall live. There's something I love even more, though, and it's the freedom to watch anything I want on TV and fart as much as I want to at any time of the day or night.

24. Therapy

I think therapy is so important and should be mandatory for everyone. I don't currently have a therapist myself, but I look forward to finding one soon. After reading this book, I'm sure you'll agree it's for the best.

25. Mom

I realized today that I only say especially nice things to my mother from a stage or when I write album liner notes or books, so I'd better not stop now. I'm very blessed to have the kind of support system I have always had in my mom (not counting the time she tried to lose me in EPCOT). She's my greatest fan and the person I love to make laugh the most (she was my test audience for much of this book). Always leading by example, she's been the one to inspire my deepest convictions about hard work, moral integrity, fairness, and basic human kindness . . . not to mention show tunes. She has been firmly by my side in my darkest hours and on my brightest days. She's the first call I make when anything happens— good or bad. When she knows I'm happy, I can hear the sun rising in her voice, and when she knows I'm not, I can hear the clouds roll in. I can also always hear the loud banging of pots and pans. For someone who claims to have so many dietary restrictions, the woman never stops preparing food.

Noisy phone calls aside, I'm so grateful to have my mom. I love her more than anyone in the world, and I want to make sure she knows that before the time inevitably comes that I murder her.

24

Bows

What are you still doing here?

This book is clearly over. . . .

I guess you really want your money's worth, huh?

Okay, well, since you're still in your seats, I suppose I might as well take my bows. That's what we'll call this little epilogue: my "curtain call." Feel free to throw roses and hotel-room keys.

Curtain calls always remind me of my grandmother. Nanny's favorite part of any theatrical performance was the end, when the company took its final bows. Of course, her favorites were the ones I took at the end of school recitals and community theater productions. But even the sight of complete strangers receiving a final ovation from their audience—even if she didn't particularly care for the show she'd just sat through—never failed to light up her eyes and fill them with tears. "Here it comes," she'd always say in wide-eyed anticipation, "my favorite part!"

I find it a little ironic (maybe "comical" is the word), seeing as how Nanny wasn't necessarily great with endings when it came to real life. When I was a little kid, she—in perfect health—famously told my parents she was concerned that I loved her too much because she didn't want me to be too upset when she eventually died, which, by the way, didn't happen until almost three decades later. Now, that's some Jewish grandmother hall-of-fame-level shit right there. When it came to the land of make-believe, however, she was all about the dramatic exit.

It wasn't until I became an adult that I really understood and began to share Nanny's emotional reaction to curtain calls. It's in those moments that you as an audience get to watch and even participate in people's dreams coming true (barring, of course, some lousy dinner theater in Newark, and no shade . . . I've been there myself). You're often witnessing their hard work—perhaps their entire lives—being validated for them right before your very eyes. That exchange is such a pure and joyful celebration. Of course, that's what she was responding to. Nanny revered show business and had great respect for anyone on a stage. Sometimes I wonder if a bit of vicarious fantasy for the arguably frustrated performer in her, who'd always secretly longed for a curtain call of her own, was creeping in and contributing to some of that light in her eyes.

I always think of those things and of her during every final bow I see or take myself. That's why I can't sit in the audience of a Broadway show without weeping during the curtain call. It's the one moment in which I am guaranteed to cry every single time. Actually, I also cry when the overture starts—that's a given. Well, I guess there is one other thing that is always sure to make me cry instantly in the theater, and that's an animal actor. Whether it's "Sandy" the dog in *Annie* or the lamb in *Gypsy*, the second I see a live animal onstage, I start sobbing uncontrollably. I don't know if it's my overwhelming love of animals or the fact that I can't believe a freakin' Pomeranian is making its Broadway debut before I do, but I lose it every time.

All the schmaltzy thoughts and theories aside, Nanny liked to see justice being served in the world at every level. I think above all, that's what the bows really symbolized to her: justice; people doing good and being rewarded for it. She, like most, knew her fair share of struggles, and as a result, she loved to see other people succeed. It takes a lot to finally get to where you're going in life in order to do what you gotta do. Elaine Stritch said it best when she quoted the proverbial prostitute on the stairs (see Chapter 8). Anyone who finally gets there in one piece deserves to be applauded, and anyone who dares to get in their way deserves to at least hear about it. I think that's also what all of Nanny's complaints ultimately boiled down to: justice.

Nanny was a serial complainer. She had a passion and a gift for it. When it came to complaining, Nanny was the GOAT (grievant of all things). She had an extensive repertoire of things that annoyed her and was never shy about presenting it. Just a few greatest hits are public displays of affection, fake or nervous laughter, unruly children, parents of unruly children, most of her friends, dieting, commercials, diet commercials, swimming pools, people who let their hair go gray, and Kathie Lee Gifford.

She could be very cynical and negative. But underneath all that cynicism and negativity was an infectious warmth and zest for life. She loved life! She complained so much only because people kept fucking it up (at least in her opinion). More importantly, even at the highest heights of her agitation, she always managed to be funny and self-deprecating. The recognition of her own occasionally irrational rants often amused her the most. She found the humor in the worst of everything, including herself, and that made her the best.

In the interest of fairness and balance, here's a brief list of some things Nanny absolutely loved: Carlo Rossi wine with an ice cube at five o'clock sharp, genuine laughter, her children and grandchildren, *Wheel of Fortune* and *Jeopardy!*, the medical profession (she was at her happiest when working or volunteering in hospitals), chocolate-covered peanuts, collecting and decorating dollhouses (her favorite hobby), watching old movies and pointing out all of the actors who had since died (her other favorite hobby), Harry Belafonte, and curtain calls . . . oh, boy, did she love those curtain calls.

As fate insisted on having it, she has not been physically present for any of the bows I've taken in over a decade (a sad fact of life about which I have many complaints). Yet somehow, I have no doubt that she's seen every last one. In any event, it's only fitting that I dedicate this and every bow I take to my favorite "kvetch comedy" artist, my Nanny. I've inherited many things from her, including what I fear may be a chronic state of aggravation. As you're now well aware, I, too, have many complaints about many things: the country, social media, even my own ass (see Chapters 10 and 12). It's only because I love life so much that I always want it to be perfect; it's constructive criticism. Life will never be perfect, though—not by my standards or yours. This world, like many of us inhabiting it, is flawed as hell, and I'm learning (very slowly) to accept that. In fact, I'm trying to embrace it. What's more, like Nanny, I will always at least try to get a few laughs out of it. What else can we do?

Okay, that's the end of my little curtain speech . . . and the end of this book (seriously this time). I really hope you enjoyed it, but if for any reason you did not, please feel free to lodge a formal complaint of your own. I can assure you, it will not reach me.

Acknowledgments

I would like to thank the following people: Victoria Varela for her unwavering support and fierce friendship; Michael Flamini for his guidance, kindness, and patience while I climbed all those proverbial stairs; everyone at St. Martin's Press for their stellar work (and for enduring my every sparkling whine throughout this process); Stacy Mark, Haley Heidemann, and my team at WME; Anthony Mattero; Bobby Quinn Rice for his star-spangled, hilarious contributions to my pretend campaign; my beloved friends and family (you know who you are).

I received many complaints from people who felt aggrieved by not being acknowledged in my last book. I would like to take this opportunity to acknowledge those people by notifying them that they will not be acknowledged in this book, either.

About the Author

Dirty Sugar Photography

RANDY RAINBOW is an Emmy– and Grammy–nominated American comedian, producer, actor, singer, writer, satirist, host, and *New York Times* best-selling author, best known for his popular web series *The Randy Rainbow Show*. His musical parodies and political spoofs have garnered him worldwide acclaim and four consecutive Emmy nominations for Outstanding Short Form Variety Series. His debut solo album, *A Little Brains, A Little Talent*, earned him a 2022 Grammy nomination for Best Comedy Album. He resides in New York City.